TENDER (n.):
A Person Who Takes Charge
Making Public Art in the Tenderloin

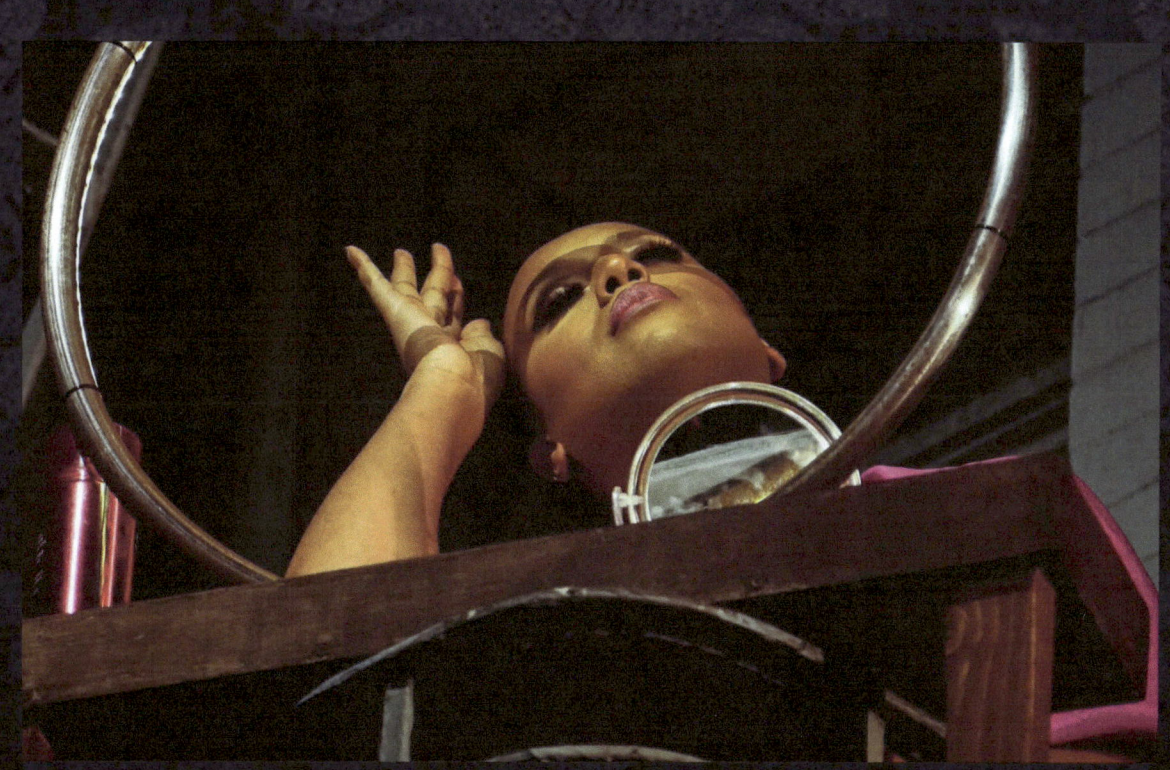

Photography: Brechin Flournoy and Austin Forbord
Page 6, Back Page, Back cover: RJ Muna
Historic photos from the Tenderloin Museum and
Pinterest – "Suffragette 1017"
Commons.wikimedia.org – "Paul Smith ca 1914"
Sfchronicle.com – "1917 Archive"
Archives.sf.weekly.com- "Soiled Doves"

TENDER (n.): A Person Who Takes Charge
Making public art in the Tenderloin

©2018 by Jo Kreiter
All Rights Reserved.
No Part of this book may be used without written permission except in the case of reprints in the context of reviews.

Flyaway Productions
1068 Bowdoin Street
San Francisco, CA 94134

ISBN-13: 978-1727791853
ISBN-10: 1727791851

www.flyawayproductions.com

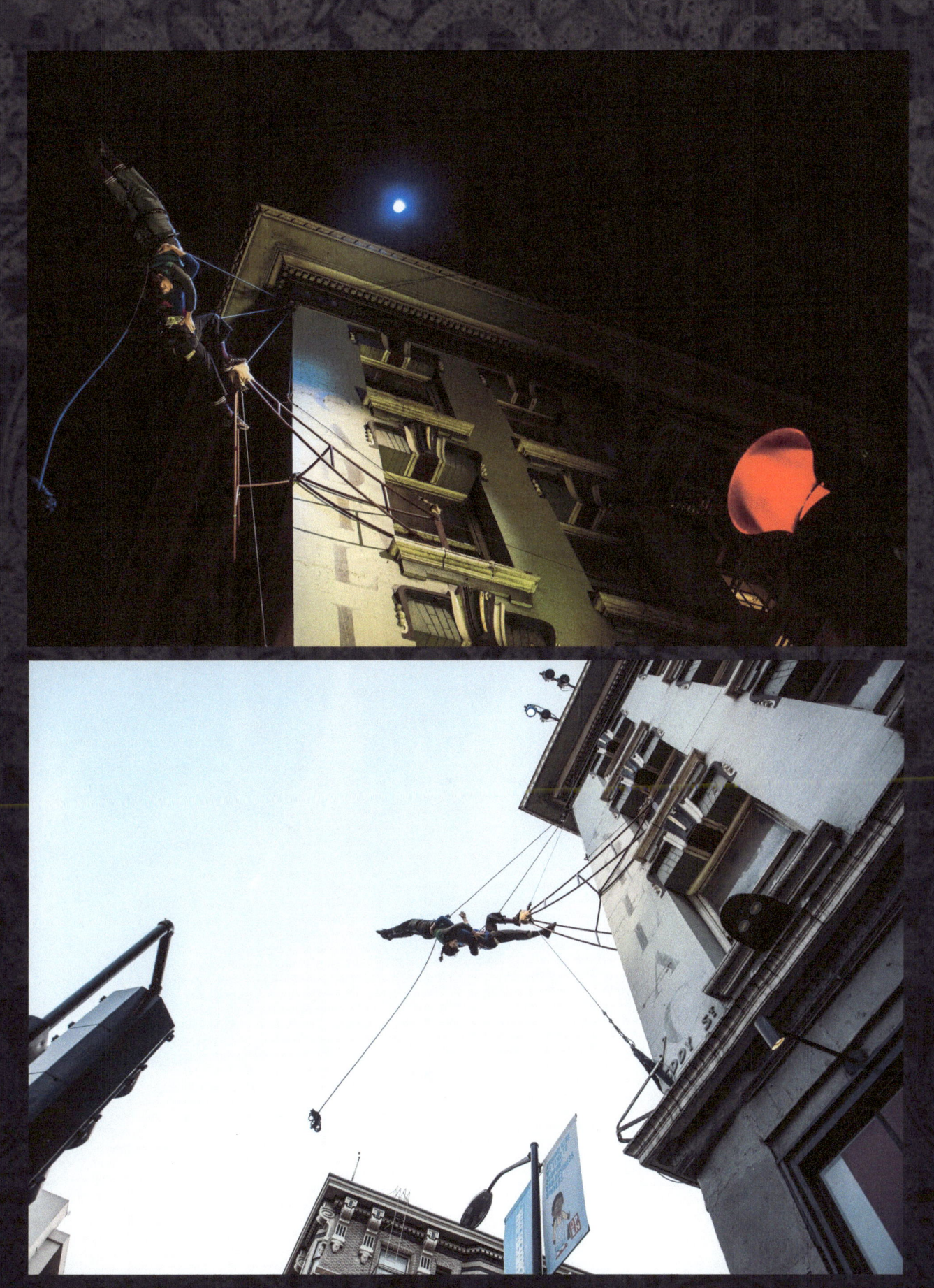

In the Tenderloin, it's been the outcasts who have stepped up, shouted, pushed forward with quiet force, taken the beatings, and refused to remain unseen. In the words of housing activist Randy Shaw, "Those fighting to prevent powerful interests from transforming the Tenderloin have included prostitutes, madams, gamblers, SRO tenants, seniors, transgender women, gay rights activists, welfare recipients, disabled persons, and Southeast Asian refugees. It's hard to believe these constituencies could overcome daily newspapers, real estate investors, public officials, and San Francisco's social and economic elite...but they did." (The Tenderloin 2015 by Randy Shaw, Urban Reality Press) Flyaway's production of *TENDER* traces one hundred years of activism in this neighborhood. It honors the outcasts, and begs the rest of us to heed their call.

- Jo Kreiter

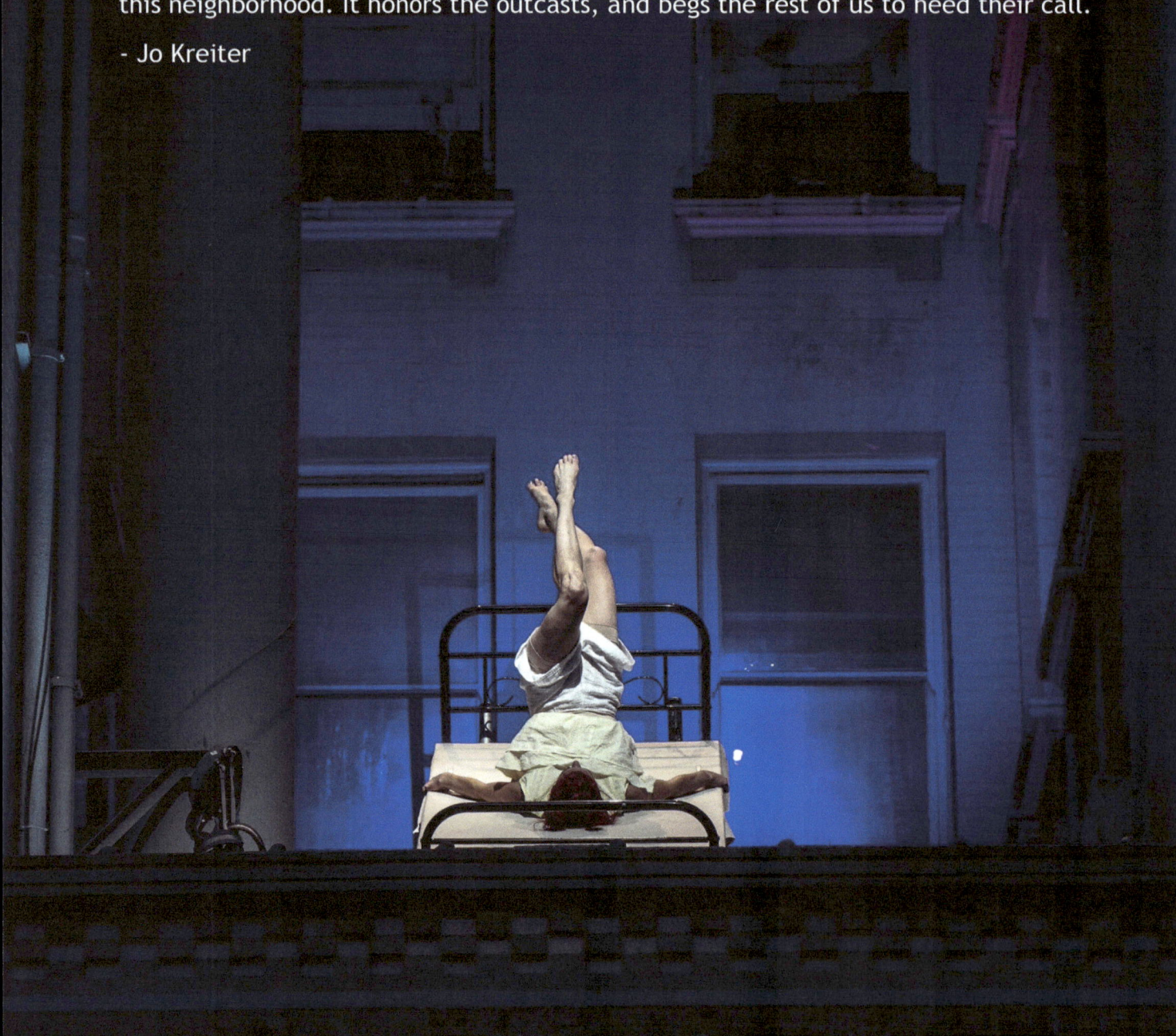

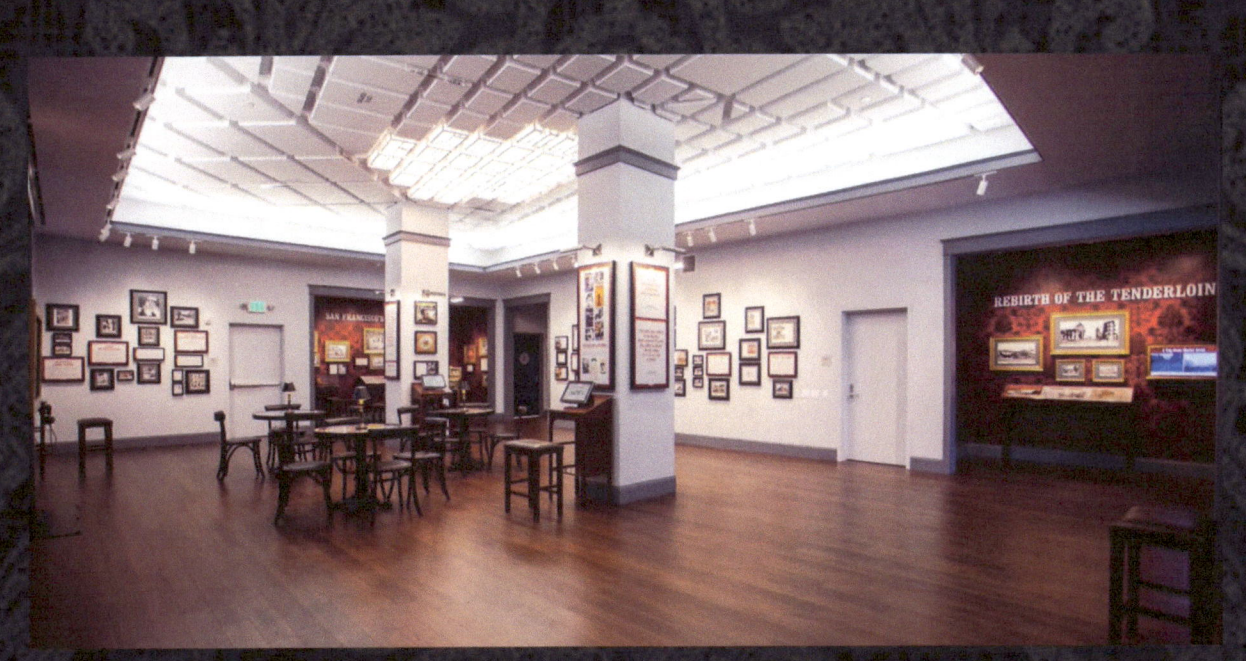

From the minute I saw Jo Kreiter's work it became my dream to collaborate with her. That dream was realized with **TENDER (n.)**. The dance integrated so many aspects of the Tenderloin Museum's mission-- amplifying the voices of marginalized populations, honoring the history of the neighborhood, and producing projects at the intersection of art, history and community.

The night before the show opened, I was looking at the museum's exhibit of working class women from the early 1900's, Then I walked outside and saw the dance inspired by these women. I was moved to tears. To see museum history leap off our walls and spill out into the streets was a deeply moving experience. And to see the history of historically marginalized groups commemorated through the spectral language of aerial dance is a powerful message to share with the public.

It was gratifying to see so many viewers not only be wowed by acrobatic dance, but also understand the connection between the dance and the history of the neighborhood. It speaks volumes about the strength of Jo Kreiter's artistry that the audience responded to the historical aspect of the performance.

The Tenderloin Museum highlights the pioneering activism and fierce resistance woven deeply into the story of our 31 square blocks. **TENDER (n.)** beautifully celebrated this history of 100 years of outcast activism, while focusing on women's history in our neighborhood.
So many residents conveyed to me how deeply the show was valued and appreciated by the neighborhood. I am grateful for what **TENDER (n.)** brought to our community, and I am honored to have been a part of it.

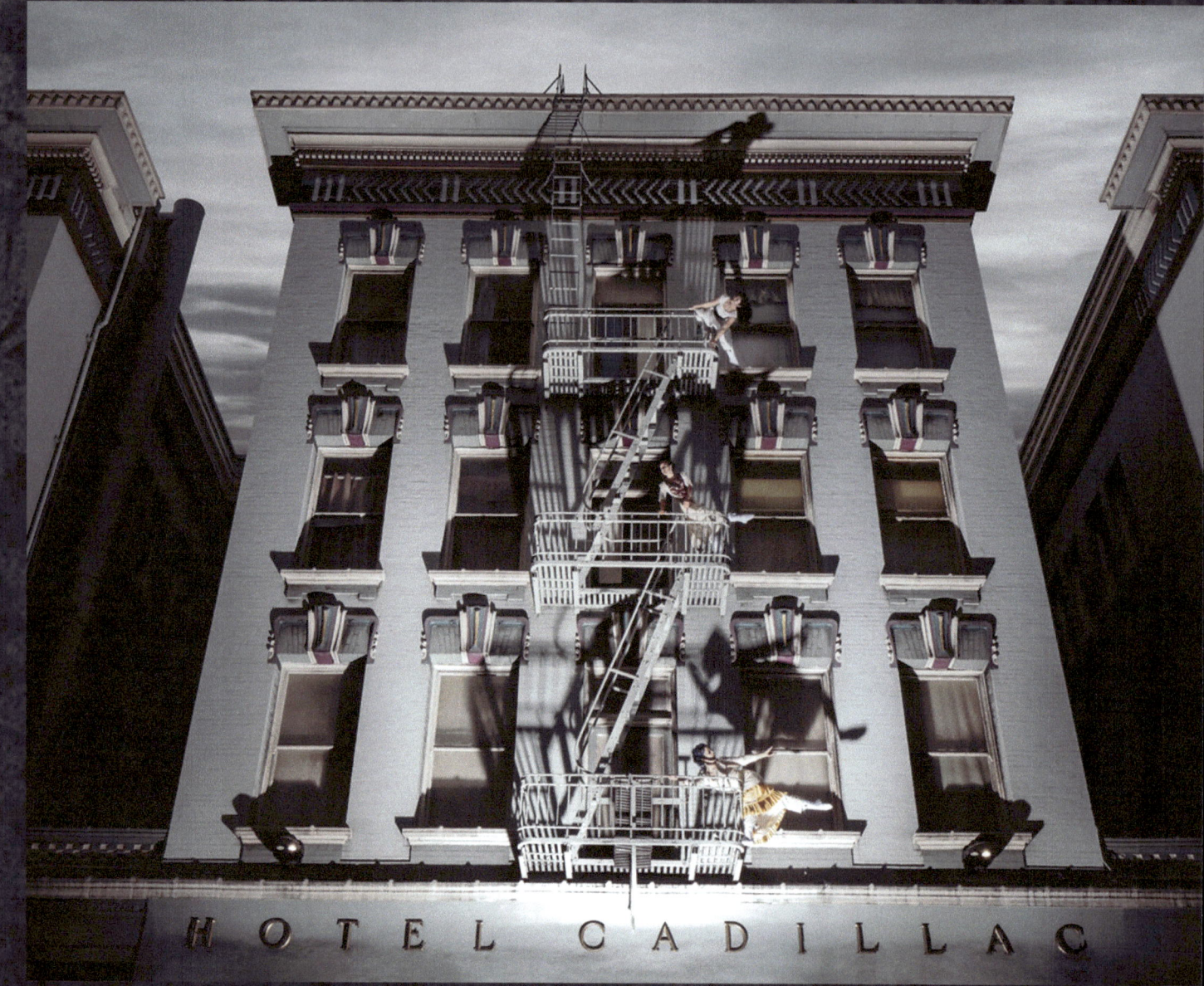

FROM THE STREET

The Street Residency starts a few months before the rehearsal process actually begins. RJ Muna, a gifted photographer who donates a lot of his time to Bay Area choreographers, joins us for a photoshoot, to get the publicity launched. Dancers Megan Lowe, Sonsherée Giles, and Bianca Cabrera spend part of a day up on the fire escape. For me, the Cadillac Hotel is such a main character in the project, that I want to create a photo that honors the architecture of the building. RJ has a vision of it on our first site visit to the street corner, so when we arrive today with his crew and Flyaway's dancers, we have a clear plan.

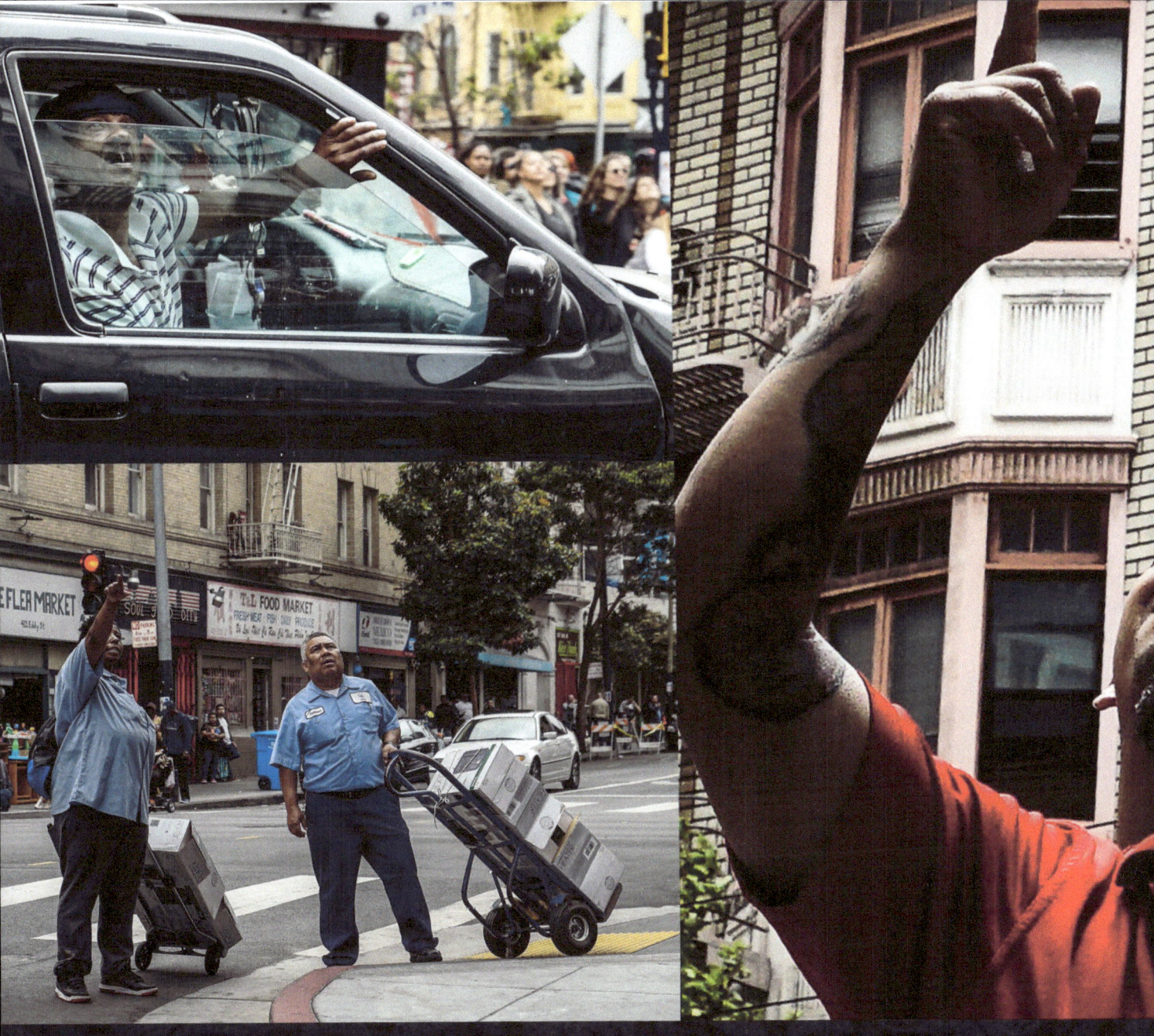

A few things happen. As we arrive, there is a man pushing a refrigerator down the street. He is also having some kind of conversation with the fridge. Two men are shouting at each other, on the verge of coming to blows. One guy drops his pants between two cars and pisses his heart out. The energy on the street is chaotic, as it often is in the Tenderloin. But as we set up and proceed to shoot, a quietness comes over the neighborhood. Even though we are playing no music. Even though the dancers are working in tableau more than movement. People gather, point, laugh, and stand wide-mouthed in awe. No one steals any equipment out from under us. One guy comes up and has a deep philosophical conversation with RJ about taking pictures. For a while, they look through the camera together. The photo shoot conjures curiosity, joy, and calm. It is a good omen for how things will go with the dance making in a few months.

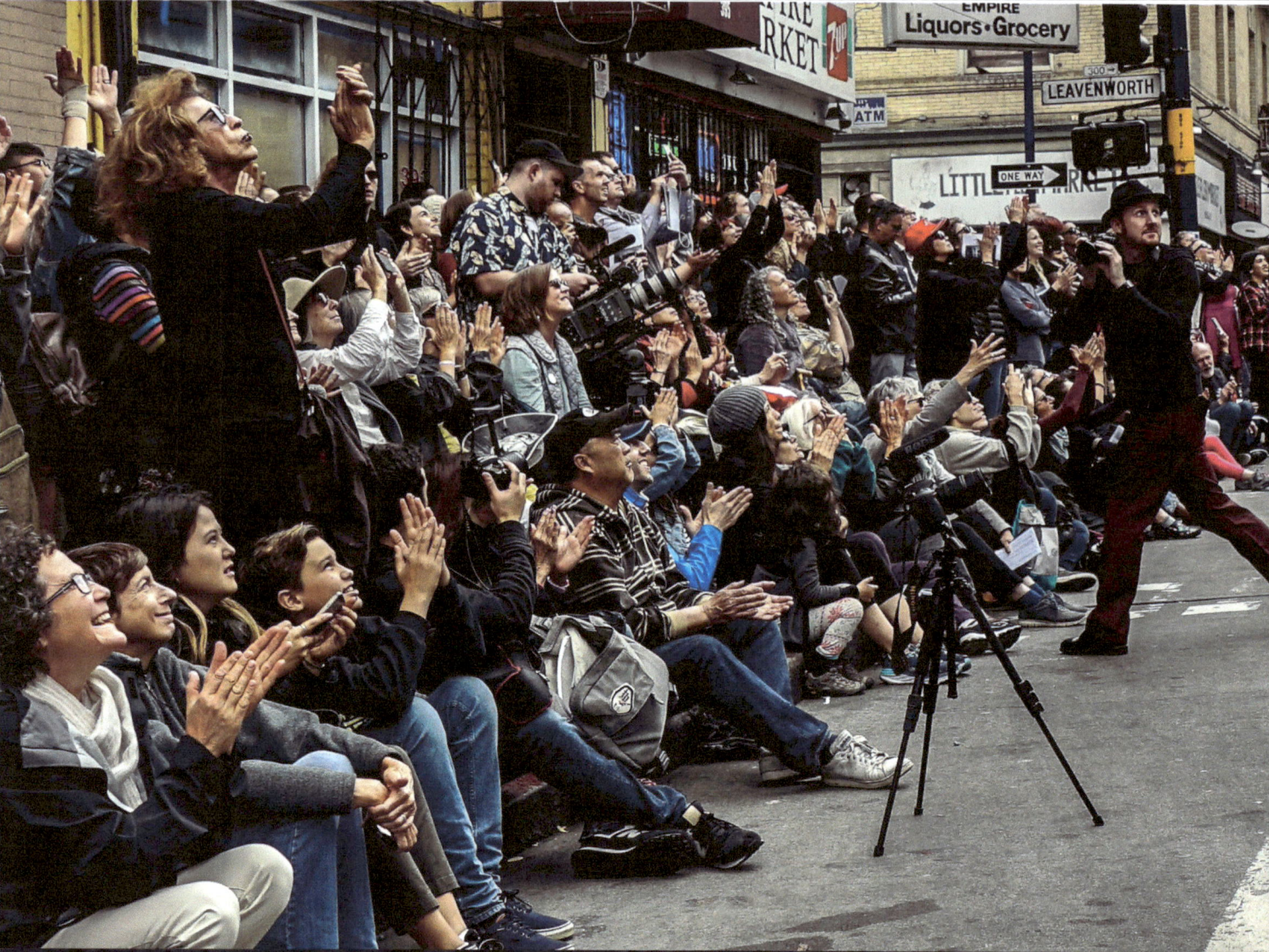

Directing this project from the street, I've met several older single women. They come up and talk to me. A few live in the Cadillac. A few live in neighboring SRO's. Their message is always the same. They tell me they don't get out much. That even getting to the street is a big effort. And they are so happy that something important is happening on their block. I've talked to at least four women in this way. Diane. Sally. I didn't catch all their names. I made TENDER for these women especially.

I have plunged into a hard negotiation with Aaron, a Cadillac Resident who is upset we are dancing outside his window. He is upset by the thump that Bianca makes each time she lands on the building. We offer him a Philz Coffee card so he can go get coffee nearby each time we are rehearsing the opening section. The Cadillac offers him another room to hang out in when we are on the wall at his window. But he is an Iraq war veteran with serious PTSD and doesn't like to leave his room. In the end, he makes his own request and we settle on washing his window in exchange for use of the air space outside of it. Problem solved. "It's a whole new world," he says, after his window is sparkling clean.

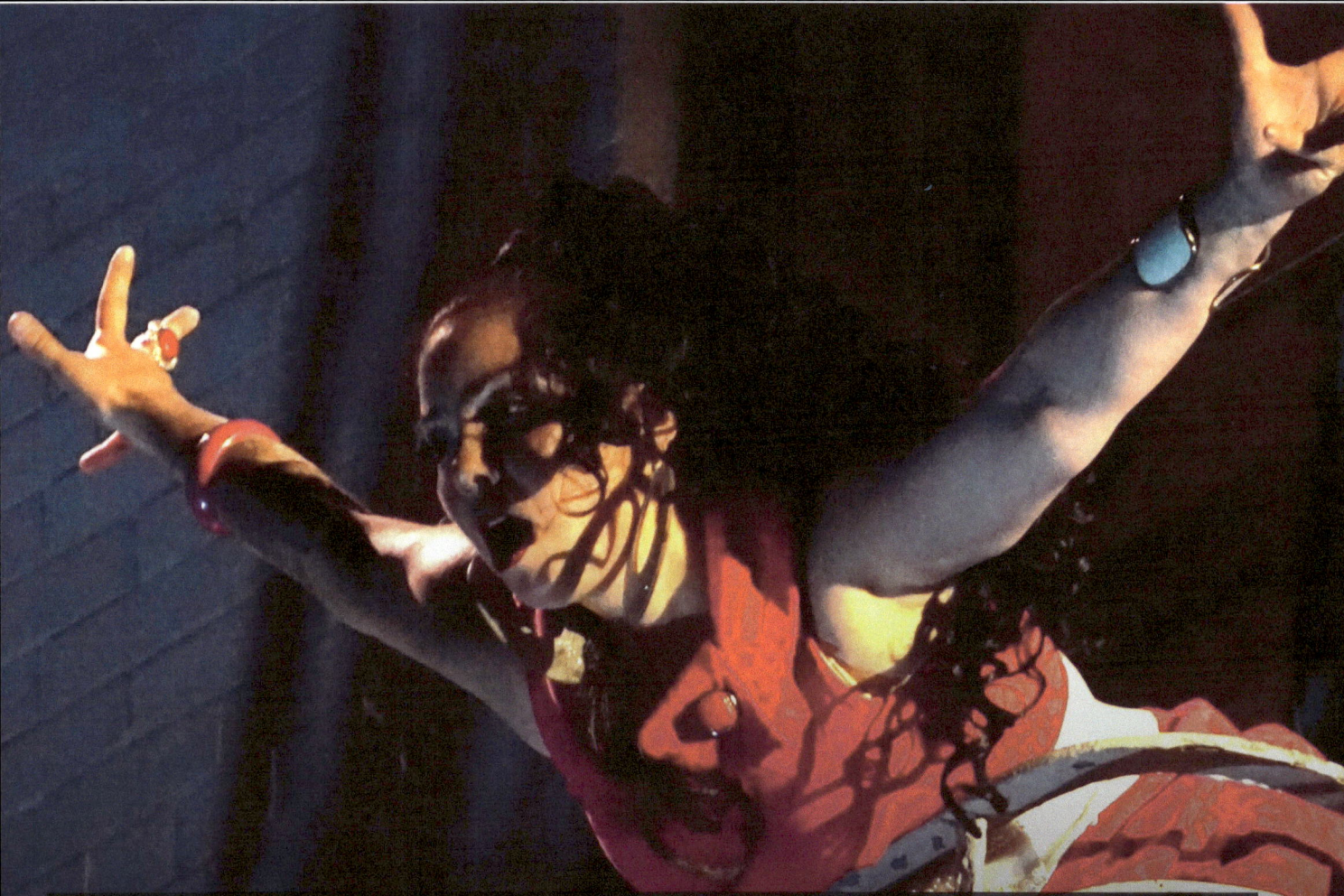

Bianca is on the third-floor fire escape balcony. She is trying out her drag queen costume. She is wearing short shorts and a false ponytail that bounces off the top of her head. She looks fantastic and is dancing the 'wild' section. A group of men gather on the street below. I think they are dealers, because of the way they cluster together like a crew, but I don't really know. I am standing on the street a few feet from them. One of them shouts up, "You for sale?" and "How much?" He is smiling and laughing. I walk over to him, tell him she's not for sale; that she's rehearsing her part for a show we are doing soon, and does he want to come see the show. We get into a fun conversation. We are both laughing. All of a sudden, a white cop comes up to him and yells, "What are you saying to her?" He is referring to me. Both this guy and I are taken aback. The force in his voice doesn't match the situation. The cop is acting like a slave owner, or a prison guard. I tell the officer that this gentleman and I are having a nice conversation. The cop stomps away. The guy and I look at each other with real confusion. "We're all good, right?" he says to me. "Yes. We're good." I say back, then I apologize. For the cop's bad behavior. For centuries of racism. What strikes me most is that whoever this guy is, he is down on his luck. His life is hard. And yet he has room in his heart to have some fun with a stranger in the street. To connect. To become interested, for a moment, in something out of the ordinary. I know his shouts up to Bianca are sexist. But the connection between he and I that followed the shouts felt worth getting past the insult.

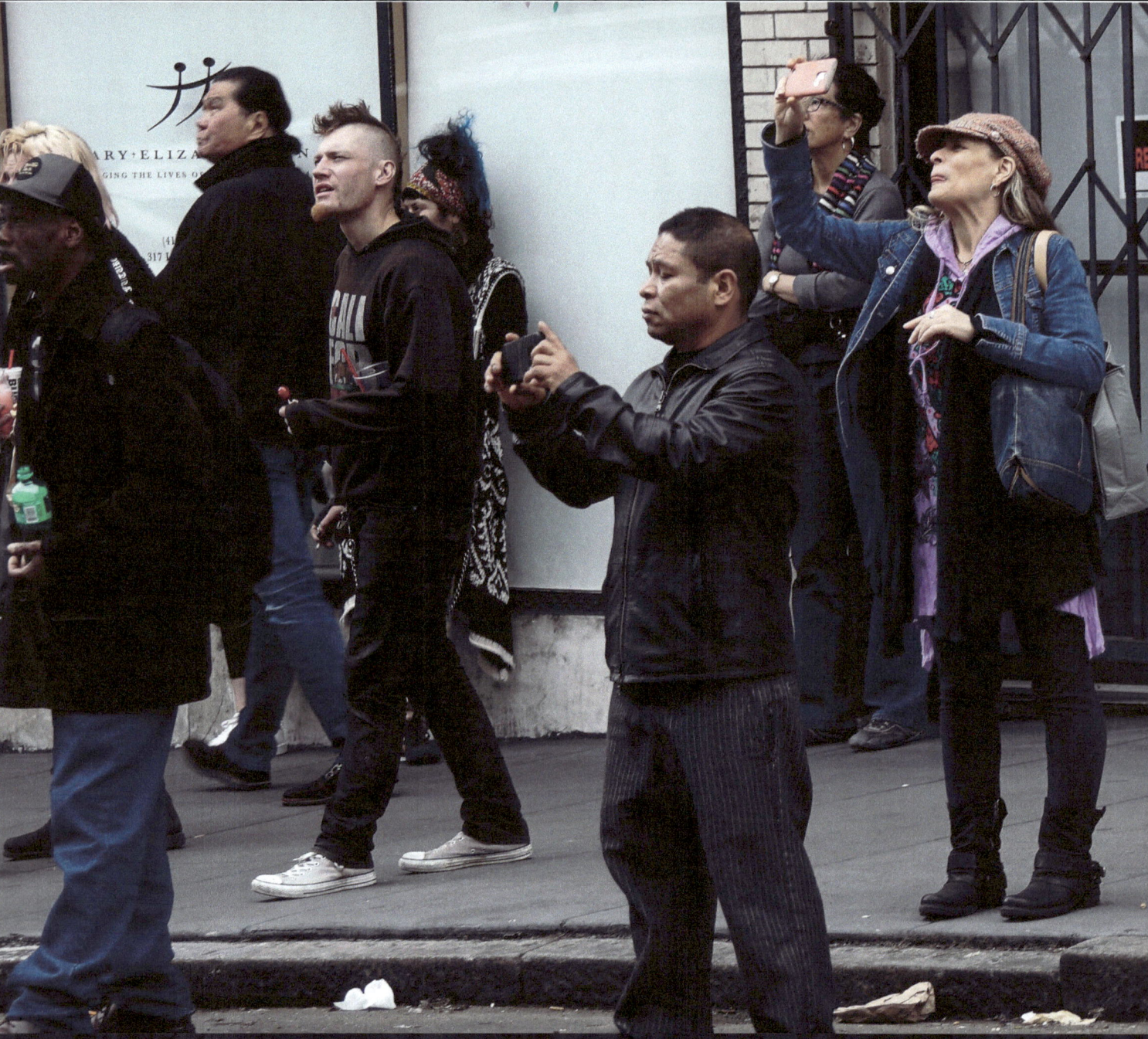

I'm standing on Eddy, directing dancers in the light well across the street. A series of sirens roll through the neighborhood, so I have to stop shouting/directing for a moment, because the sirens drown out my voice. A woman is standing next to me. She asks me why I've stopped shouting out. I tell her the sirens make it so the dancers can't hear me. Somehow, we come around to talking about violence in the neighborhood. She says that people try to make out like all the city's gunshots happen in the Tenderloin, but they don't. "Don't get me wrong," she says, both smiling and dead serious, "I know a lot of shit goes down here." But the gun deaths aren't on us. And when they do happen, it's from people that don't even live here." "Point taken," I say. Today I learned just a little bit more about what it is to defend your neighborhood.

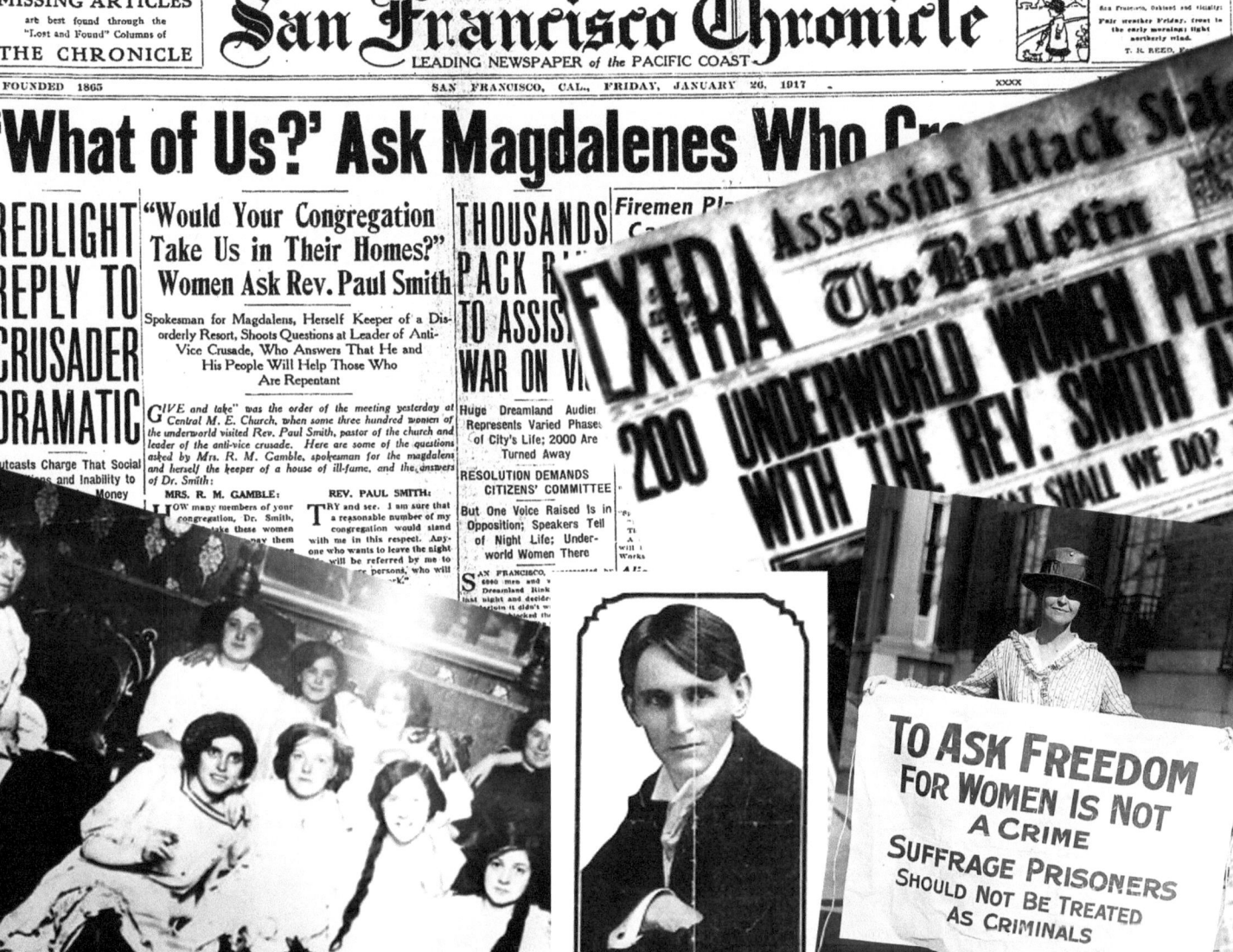

LADIES DANCING

In 1917, the Tenderloin was thriving. It hosted mostly single, childless, white collar workers seeking affordable rent and a fun nightlife. It had six street cars connecting it to the rest of the city. It was a hub for working class, unmarried women, because it was close to the stores on Market Street where they worked. But the neighborhood came under siege by people like Reverend Paul Smith, who couldn't stand seeing women have fun without men's permission. Moral Reformers succeeded in shutting down the neighborhood, barring single women from travelling freely into bars and clubs and going where they wanted to. But not without resistance. And not for long. The coming era of prohibition changed the neighborhood back toward wildness once again.

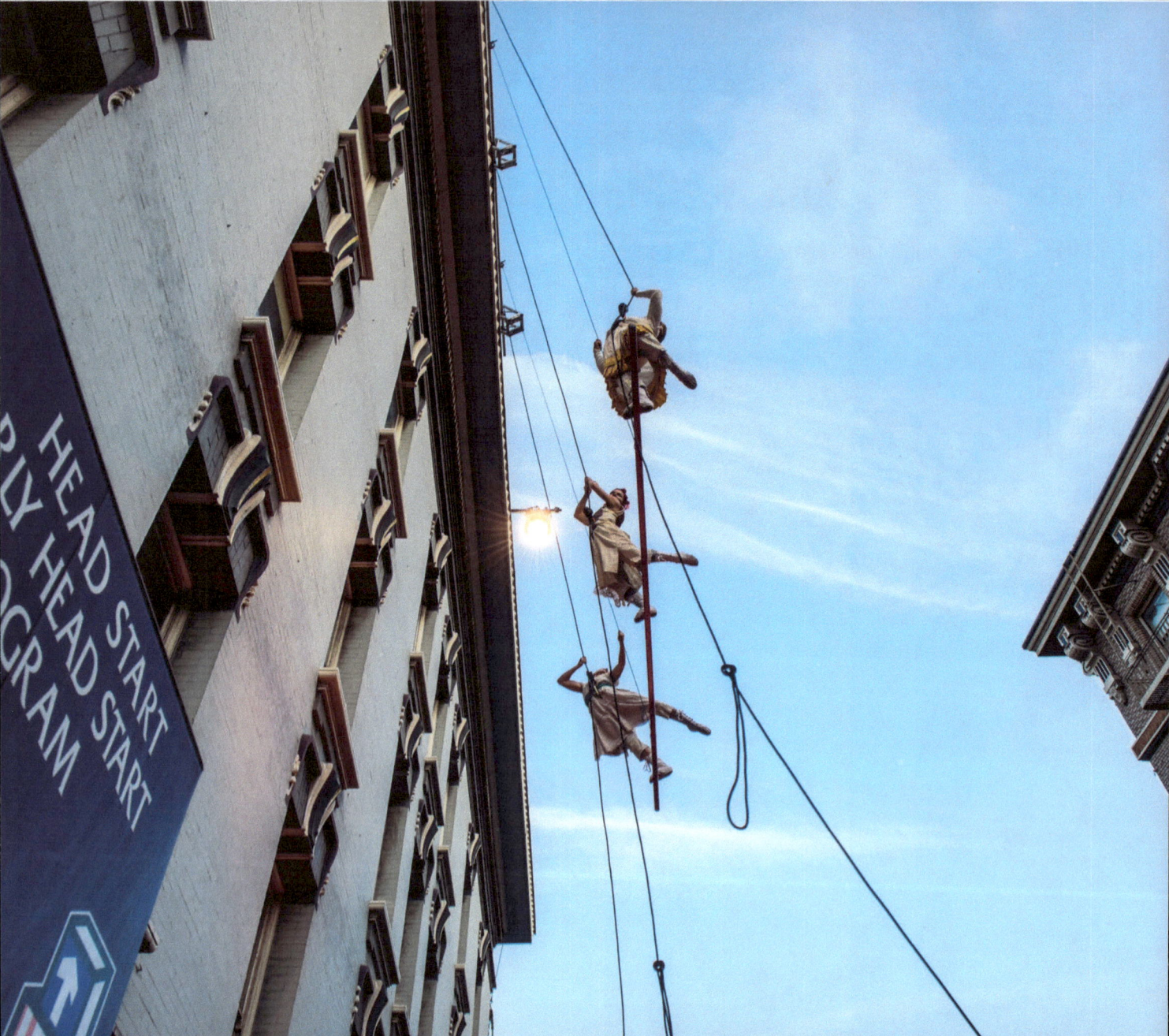

I stand on the corner at Eddy and Leavenworth. It's here I can see what is happening on both sides of the building. I'm watching the trio get situated on the wall. The dancers adjust the choreography to accommodate the window ledges of the building. They are getting used to the height of the red pole we have suspended from the roof. Because of the overhang, the 20-foot pole hangs three feet out and away from the building. The dancers work with it as a giant swing that creates unity of time and space as they magically fly into the sky and back toward the building. A thick red pole is the base of the swing. It represents the street of 100 years ago—when it was radical to walk on the sidewalk unaccompanied by a man; when it was radical for women to work and live outside of their family homes.

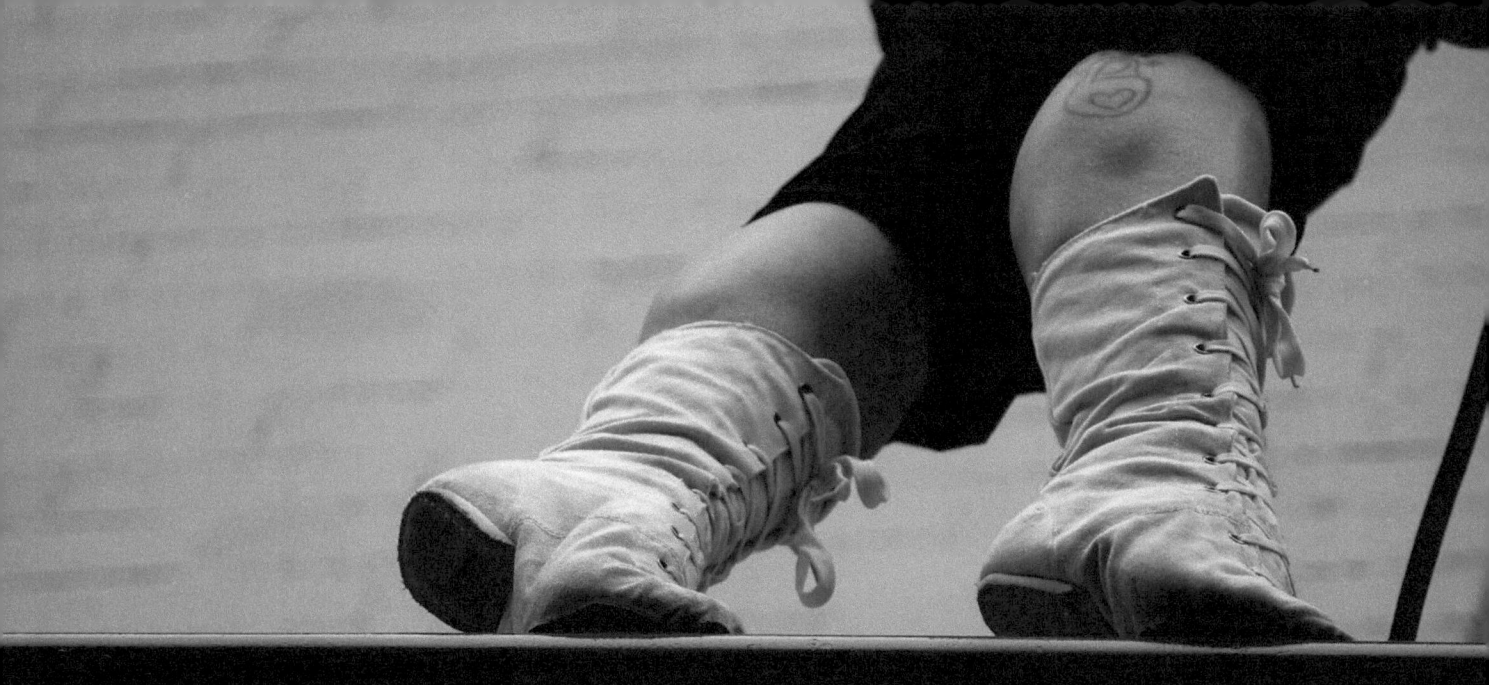

The dancers are setting their timing to the music. I asked our composer, Vân-Ánh Võ, to work with pop songs from 1917, and she has masterfully inlaid music from the era with sounds of women walking on the street, laughing, and drinking in bars. I've chosen to focus the choreography on the animal dances of the time…the fox trot and the grizzly bear dances…reinventing them into an aerial vocabulary. The effect is both haunting and delightful.

As I watch, I am transported 100 years back in time—and also heavily aware of some neighborhood women camped out on the sidewalk below and just to the right of the dancers. For now, it's their place to sit. Be left alone. No one is asking them to get up and move. This sidewalk is their living room, den, kitchen, and bed. Above them we are conjuring the history of the women who walked this sidewalk 100 years ago. Some of them worked in shops. Some of them worked for madams.

In 1917, at a significant protest at the Methodist church at Leavenworth and O'Farrell (two blocks from where the dancers are rehearsing), a posse of women of the underworld, led by Madame Gamble, challenged the status of women by saying, "Men here in SF say they want to eliminate vice. If they do, they better give up some of their dividends and pay girls wages so they can live…" (The Tenderloin 2015 by Randy Shaw, Urban Reality Press).

It amazes me that we are still working to transform the patriarchal dividend

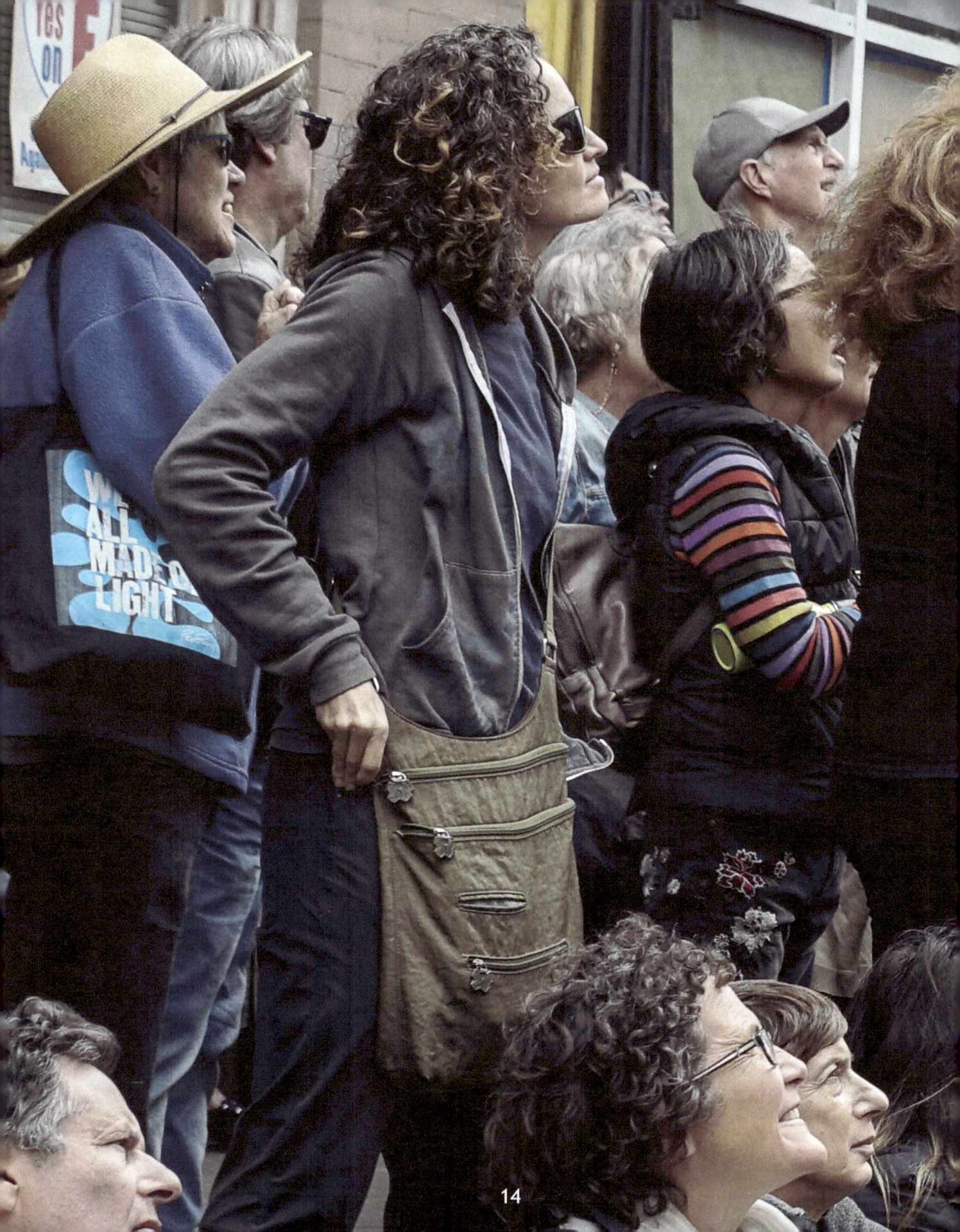

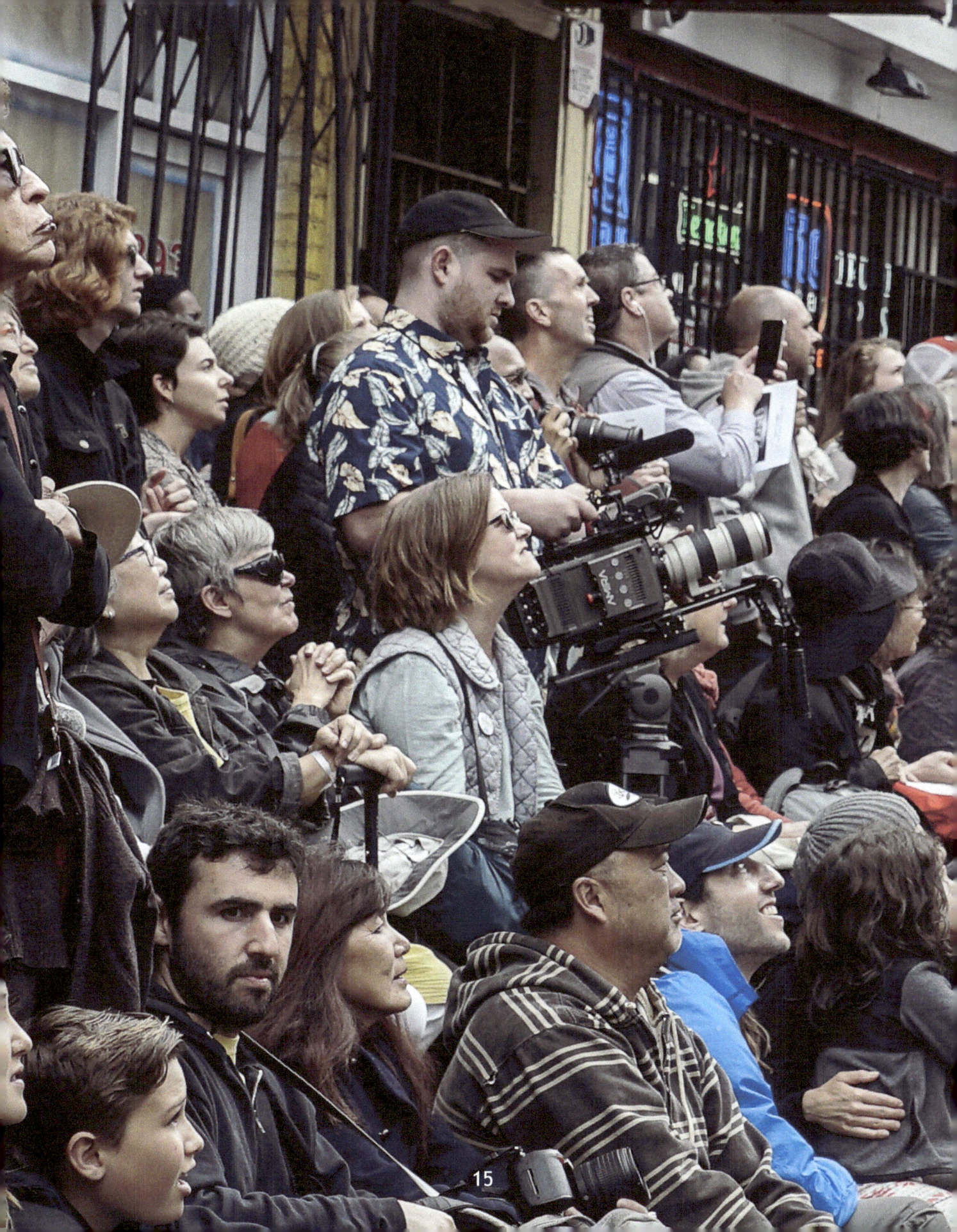

Seeing Flyaway Productions' dancers performing *TENDER* on the Cadillac Hotel was one of the most memorable moments in my life! Seeing them skip, hop, turn, and twirl all the while telling the story of the Tenderloin through dance and music was, for me, a life changing moment. I was literally holding my breath the whole time—all the while hoping no one would fall, but at the same time being transfixed and breathless by the beauty of it all. I almost didn't want to blink in case I missed a single second!

The dancers evoked the feeling that we were watching history being made in our very own community. And we were watching history—the Tenderloin's history. We were also hearing the life stories of several of our residents as a part of the story/dance/music performance.

Flyaway brought new life and vigor into our centuries old and tired neighborhood. You brought us hope—that there will always be art and beauty in our lives. Thank you for helping us transform our little neck of the woods into a destination for all brave creative and artistic souls!

Kathy Looper
Owner, the Cadillac Hotel

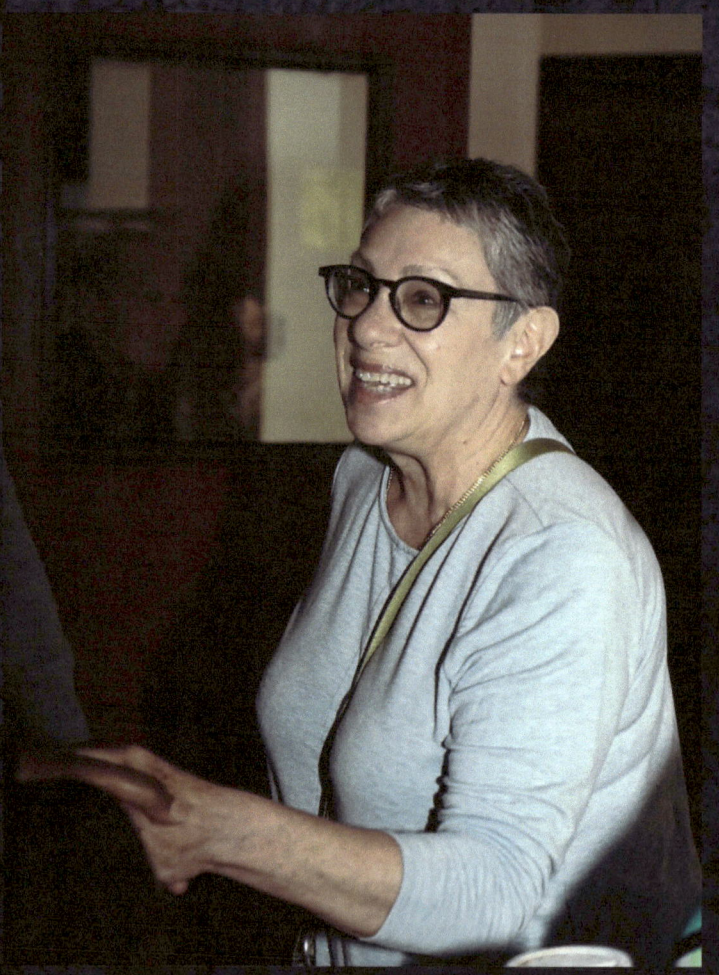

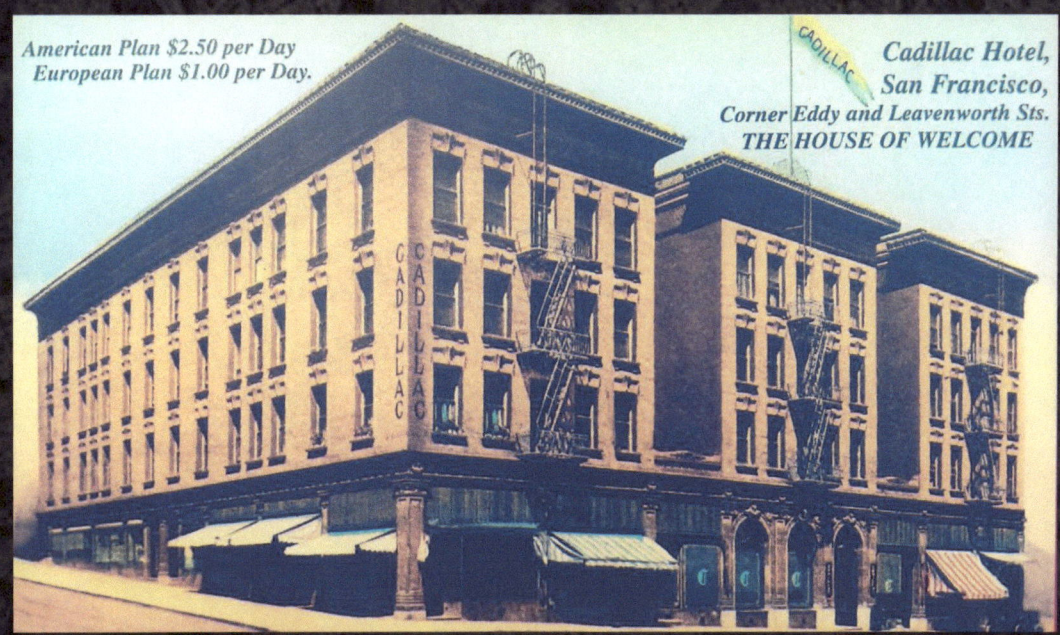

TENDER's timeline starts in 1917, and ends in 2018, with a focus on housing. When I plan the final section of the piece, I call it **Kathy's Dance.** In the 22 years that I have been making dances on buildings, *TENDER* is only the second project I have created for a building that is owned by a woman. The other is The Women's Building in San Francisco's Mission District. We danced there in 2010, to celebrate its centennial.

1977 was the year Kathy and Leroy Looper bought the Cadillac Hotel. They bought the hotel because they wanted to make the Tenderloin a safe and affordable place to live, especially for people living through addiction and recovery. Although Leroy passed away in 2011, this is still Kathy's goal today.

The ground floor of the Cadillac has been a boxing ring where Muhammed Ali made an appearance, a liquor store called the Ringside, and a Sizzler restaurant. Now it's the home of the Tenderloin Museum.

Composer Vân-Ánh Võ and I interview Kathy as part of our Cadillac Hotel residency. What becomes clear to me, almost immediately, is how much Kathy cares about the work and life she built around the Cadillac. She raised four kids here and has dedicated the better part of her adult life to its residents. But Kathy demurs the spotlight. She doesn't think of herself as an activist (though I certainly do). She talks about how Leroy walked into a bank way back when to get a loan for the building and got it, because it was a time when banks were actually involved in real revitalization. But she doesn't talk about herself much, except to say how much it means to her to bring art into the Cadillac community. She sees art as part of an antidote to poverty.

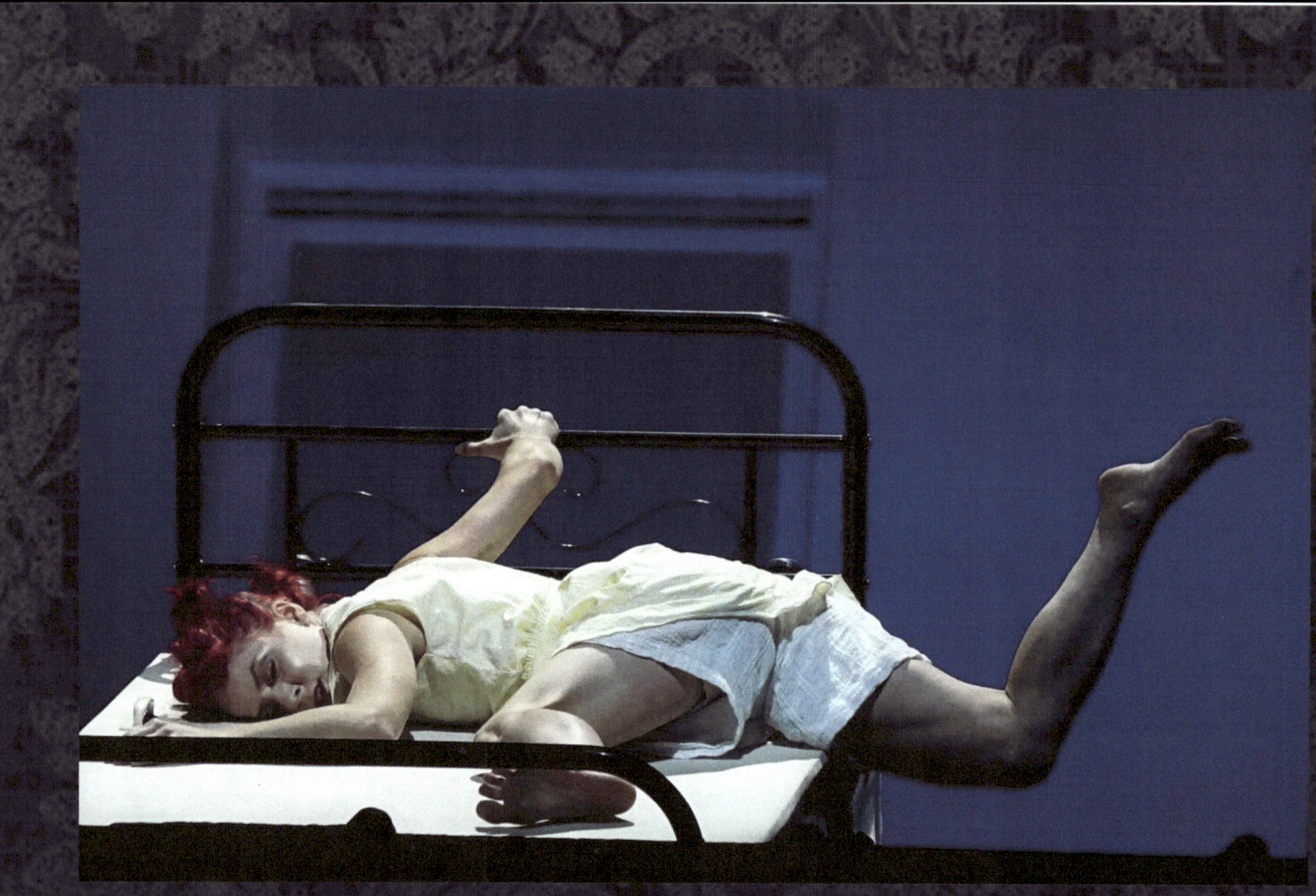

Learning this, I decide to focus the finale on the Cadillac's residents. We interview several people and choose to center the section on Mary's story. Her voice starts the finale: *"It's three o'clock in the morning… I was dope sick…"* She tells the audience how she was sick on the street outside, below the Cadillac, and dreamed of a 4th floor corner room as her own. Within months, she got clean and made it so. She now lives in that 4th floor corner room.

Everyone at Flyaway makes a deep connection with Mary. I have bonded with Mary because we have both lived as wives of an incarcerated loved one. Her husband comes home from the state penitentiary in 2023 and she is waiting. I understand her wait. During the residency, she visits with Megan and Yayoi Kambara on the boat every day. They are dancing right outside her bedroom window. She also checks in with Bianca every day. They have gotten especially close. Mary comes downstairs at the change-over between sections to help the dancers dress into their second costumes. Or she waits upstairs by the balcony for Bianca. She knows Bianca's cues; knows when Bianca stops for water before running up the stairs and is nearly late for her entrance. Bianca tells me that during the finale, when Mary's story is being danced for audiences, she gathers her six dogs on her bed. They huddle together and listen. They are sweet together. Vulnerable. And proud as well.

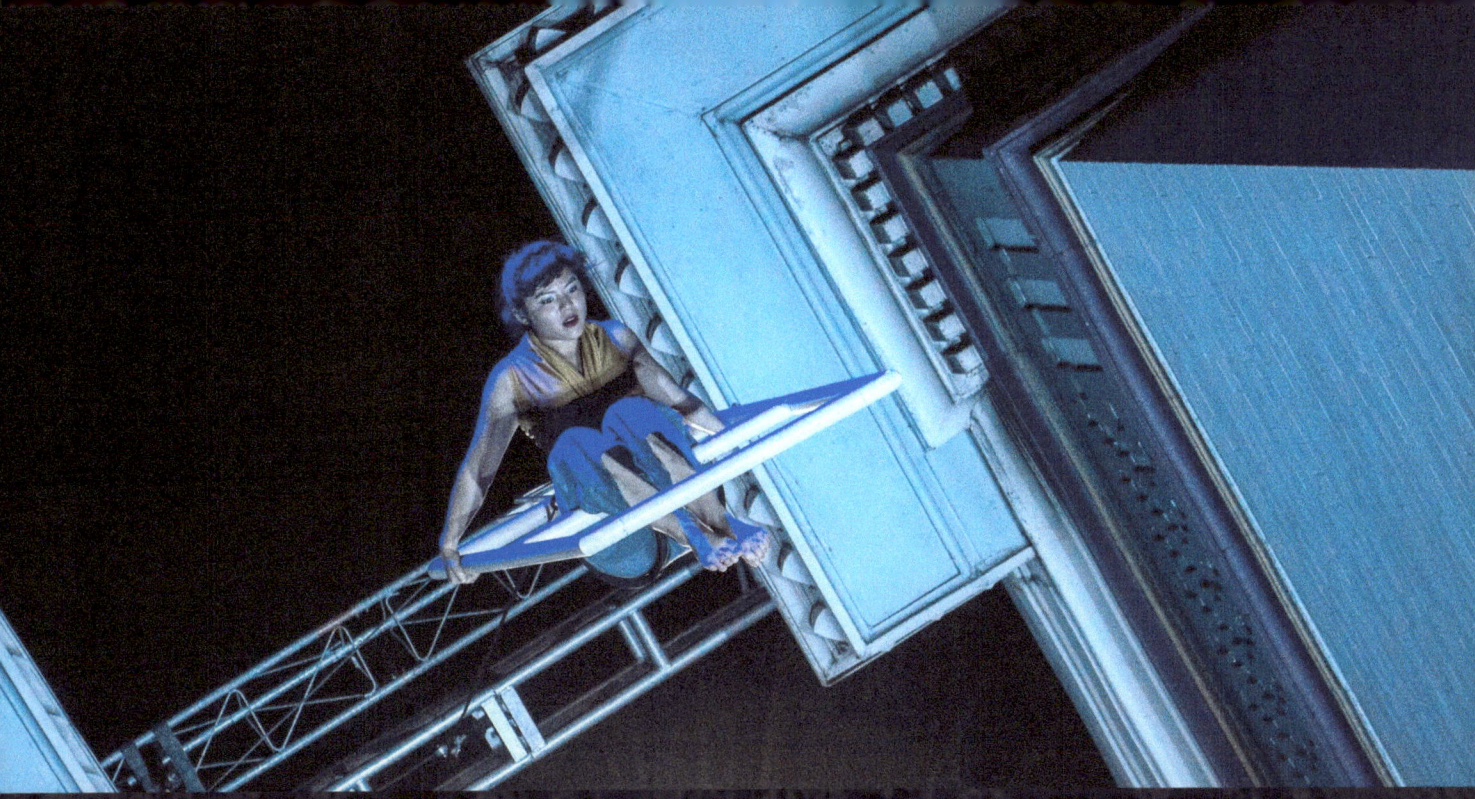

The Cadillac is a building with stark contradictions. Its relative safety, and its windows out onto the street are a source "of light and great joy," according to Dave Anderson, who has lived there for three years. But its walls, peeling paint, and brick are also a reflection of disappointment for many who live there. There is piss in the hallways. Empty liquor bottles. Broken glass. Slamming doors. An odor of sorrow. There is, in resident Mark Parson's words, "the beauty of a building that once was..."

In the light well of the building, we place the final set pieces for the performance. The dancers can only get there from the roof, rappelling in from a rope. I design a trio for a bed, a rope, and a window suspended in the center of the light well. The rope allows MaryStarr Hope to swing from side to side of its narrow span. The window is made to match the actual windows of the building. Megan activates the window like an urban trapeze, swinging precariously out over the street and back again toward the back side of the well. Her performance embodies the best of what dance has to offer. She releases and catches, again and again. Her body in space is seemingly wild, but also utterly in control. As you watch, she thrills you, and scares you a little. Below her, about 20 feet off the ground, Sonsherée is dancing on a narrow bed. Her presence is evocative in a different way. She reminds you of how precarious it is to have a bed to sleep in, if you are lucky enough to get off the street and into an SRO hotel. The dancers fill you with awe that someone (though its actually an entire team of riggers, designers, technicians, dancers, and a choreographer) has bothered to imagine something infinitely beautiful, in a neighborhood that swelters with pain

BUILDING A COALITION

The Au Co Vietnamese Cultural Center. The Tenderloin Museum. The Cadillac Hotel. The Asian Art Museum. CounterPulse. Code Tenderloin. Flyaway Productions. We are artists, activists, survivors of war, keepers of history. We live on the streets or just off of them. We are the coalition of *TENDER*. We each have a vital role in the project. *TENDER* advances our capacity to be a part of coalition building toward social justice.

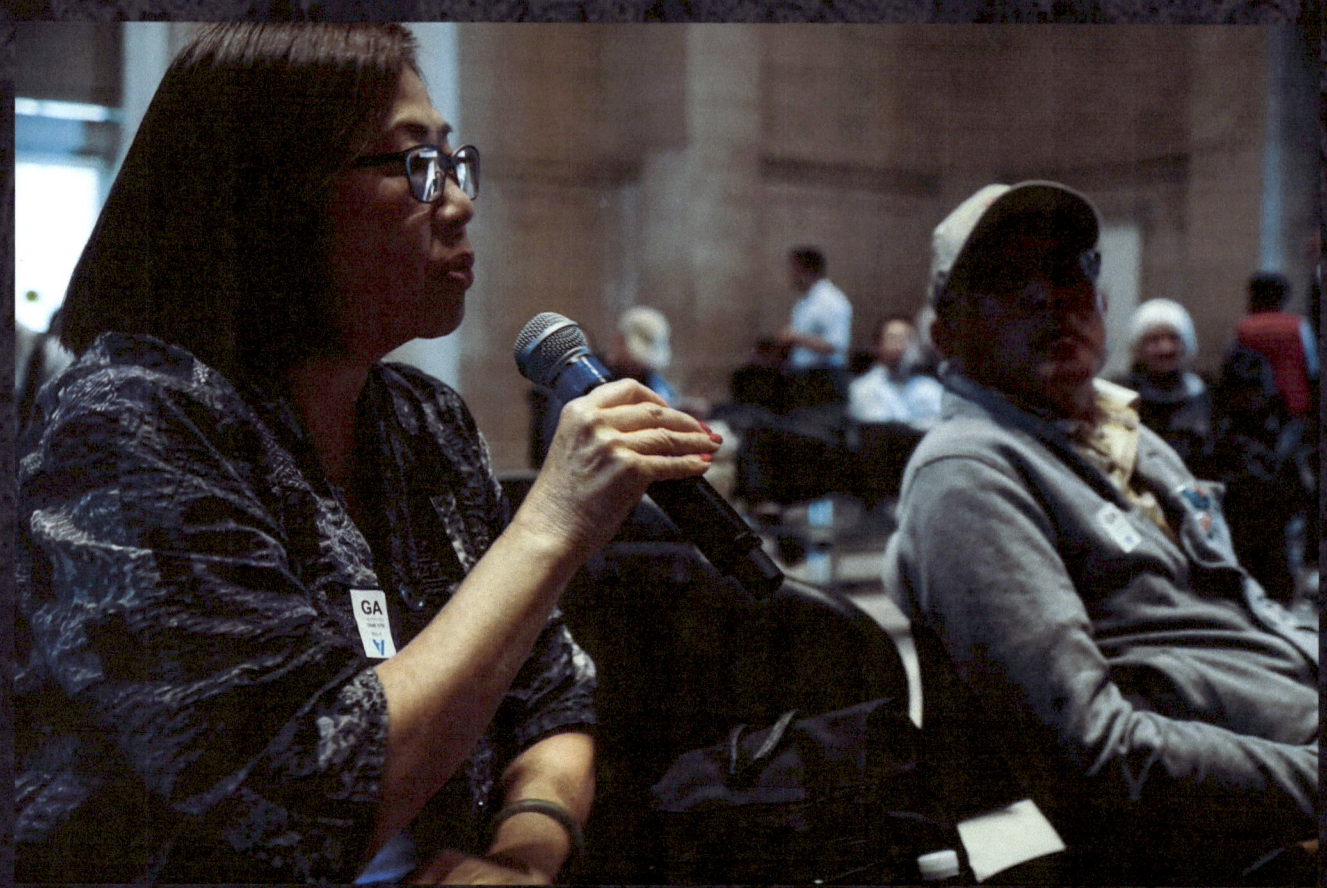

Au Co Center Director Hang To gathers together a group of South Asian residents of the Tenderloin. They share their experience of arrival to the U.S., and to the crowded streets of the Tenderloin. Karen Tieu is especially articulate about her journey on a boat away from the "American War." She speaks of raising her family in the cramped spaces of neighborhood housing in the Tenderloin. In "This Boat," we tell the story of her journey. Vân-Ánh makes the music in two sections: stories of the boat people, and stories of living in the neighborhood. Her composition of the second section of music is so cheerful. I ask her about it when I hear it the first time. Her answer stays with me: "I want the music to be happy. My community cannot stay in trauma forever."

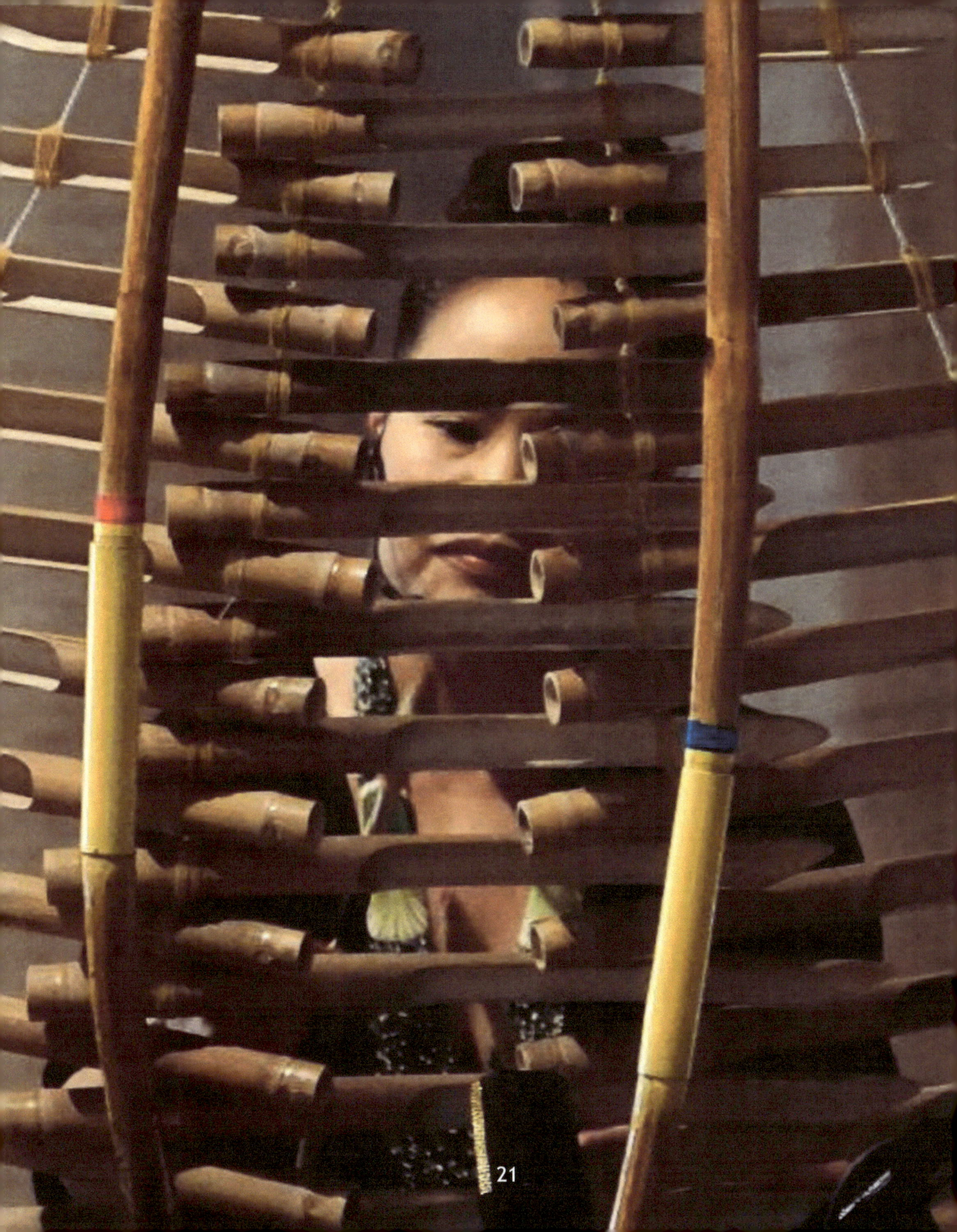

The Asian Art Museum introduces the project to its audiences a few months before the street residency begins. They also organize, with the Tenderloin Museum, two walking tours that help viewers situate the project into a wider historical lens.

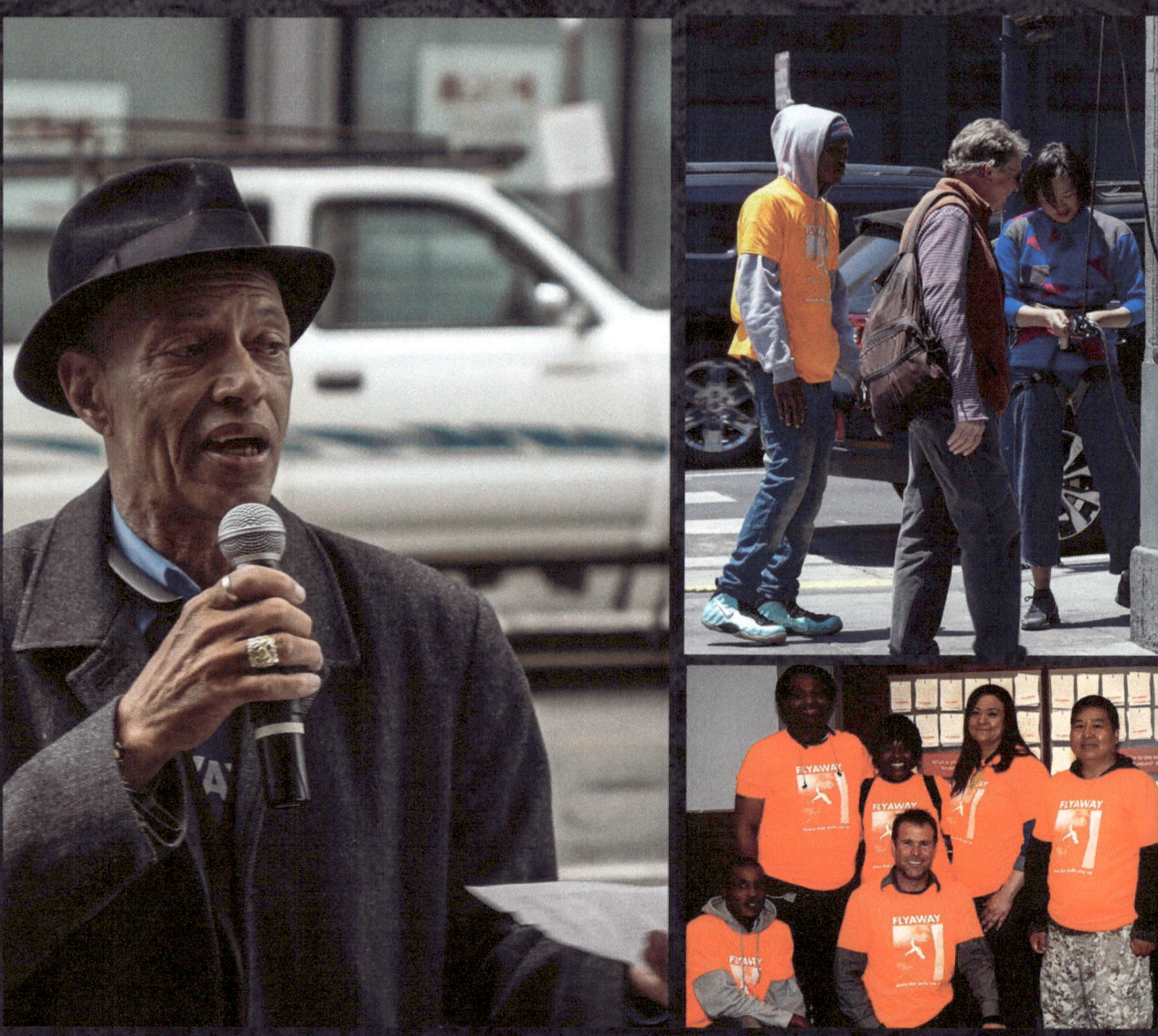

There is Del Seymour, Code Tenderloin Founder, and his team. Each night we hire people from Code Tenderloin to greet the audience, and support their experience. Justice, also known as J, introduces the history to audiences before each show. Del does the introductions for the matinees. Del and J know the painful side of the streets, having lived through its drug culture and come out the other side. Including their voices in the project gives it heft. The whole Code Tenderloin team has a way of inviting audiences into the experience of watching the piece that puts people at ease. This is a skill that comes from knowing street culture, and being of it.

WHY IT HAS TO BE ART

When I was a political science major at Duke, I studied coalitions in the U.S., Latin America, and Africa that brought about significant political change. I've modeled my arts organization's coalition building on the ideals and effectiveness of civil rights movements whose participants work primarily in the political realm. As a dance artist, I've chosen to layer in the motional body as an additional, essential catalyst for social change.

In *TENDER* we dance in an extremely disinvested area of the city, where drugs are rampant and too many people live in the margins, often unhoused. We dance on a building with a large overhang, which brings extreme engineering challenges that we meet with rigging ingenuity and safe design. We power the piece with generators on two roofs and a battery operated, mobile cart on the street. We integrate character, momentum, invention, four changes of costumes, new apparatus, and a charismatic drag queen into the work, expanding our vocabulary and theatrical span. We work with a world-renowned composer who has never composed for dance. Our greatest challenge is the emotional and psychic drain that comes from working at ground zero for America's poverty crisis. It's difficult to be creative amidst the sorrow, rage, and desperation that permeates the street. We dance on a building that people live in, bringing dance right into people's living rooms, literally. This project raises the bar for how dance can be relevant in people's day to day lives.

TENDER began with a call to action from Tenderloin housing activist Randy Shaw. He has repeatedly called out for a neighborhood where low income folks can feel safe walking at night; where people can afford to live; and where people are proud to call home.

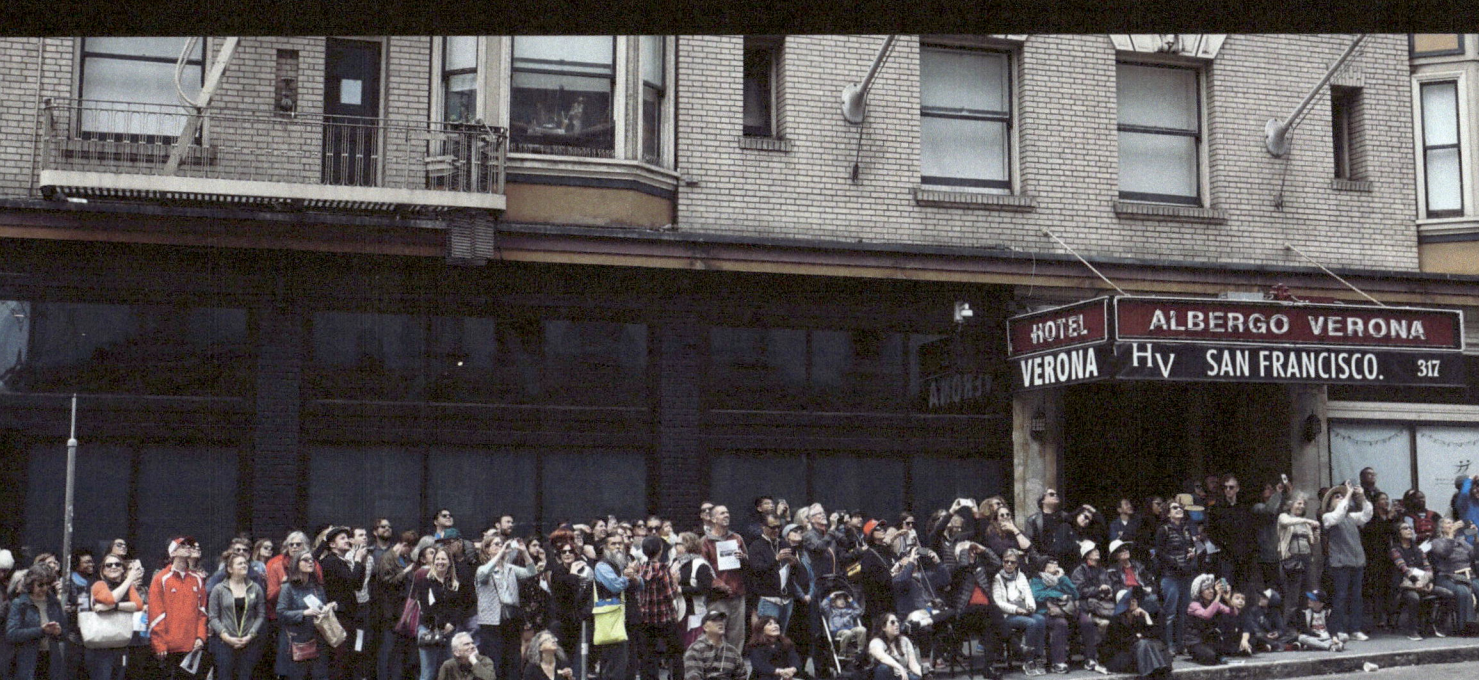

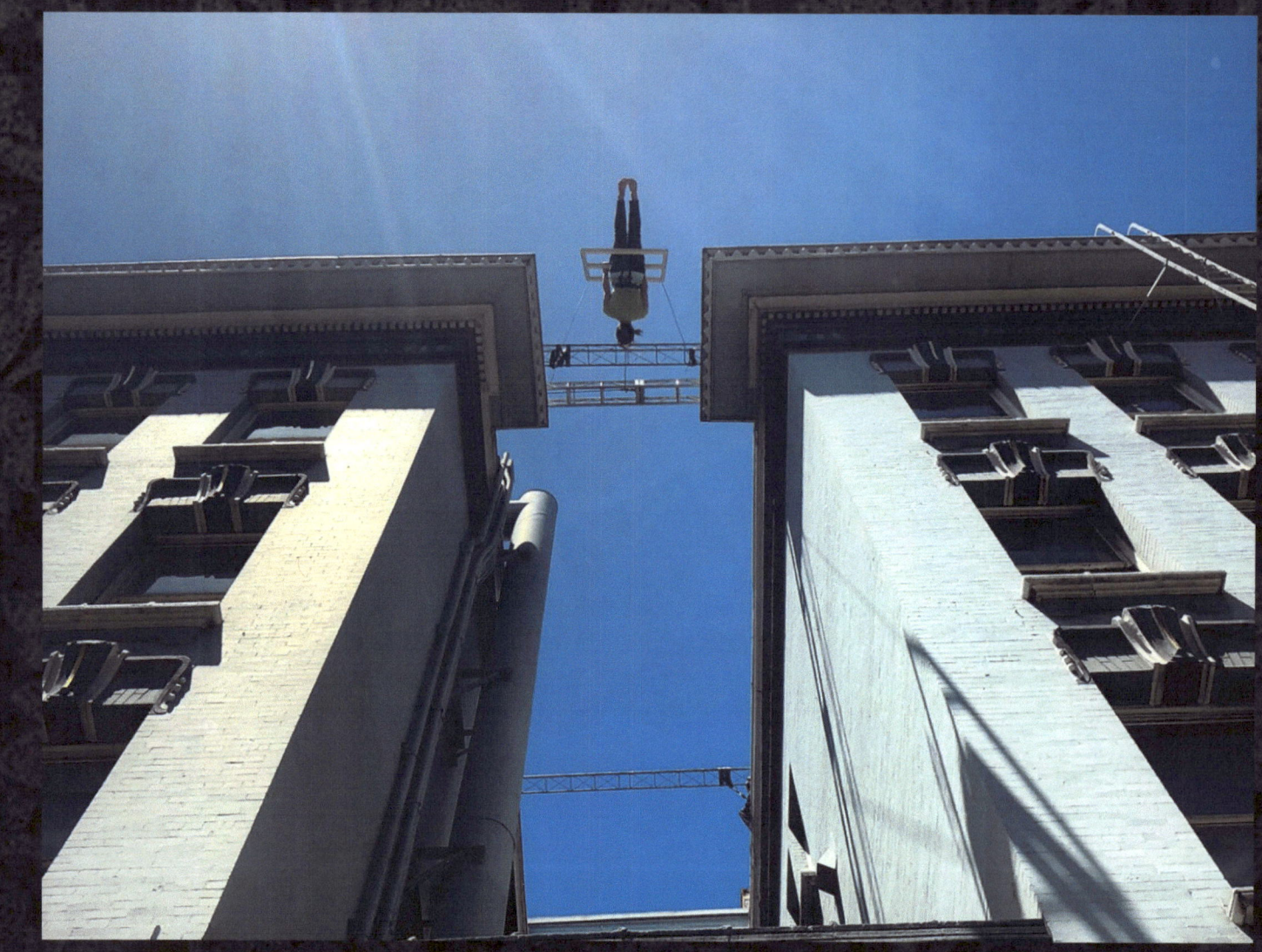

Mark Parson lives at the Cadillac. He has been coming out and watching rehearsals every few days. We interviewed him for the project, but his voice doesn't make it into the piece, though he is quoted in the program. Tonight, he comes out and sees the lighting go up on the dancers during our first technical rehearsal. It's impossible to describe the enchantment on his face when he sees the magic: *"I feel like this is real theater and it makes my life here mean something."*

There is often an unspoken expectation that community-based art comes with lower artistic standards. I've spent 22 years defying this. Defiance is in the sleek design of objects, startling pools of light, the whirl of rich costume textures. It's in the unimaginable twists of a dancer's body as she swings above the street lamps and electric wires. Both wild and immaculate artistry are crucial to site-specific public art, if it is to be a part of the fabric of social change. To be uncompromising in the creation is to honor the depth of the struggle that has brought us to the streets in the first place.

I feel a deep obligation to harness accurate, socially relevant information, holding myself accountable to the women whose stories I am telling, with hope that the telling will shift their burden. In *TENDER*, we wrap the building with four distinct dances. In laced white boots; on the prow of a steel boat rigged to the building's corner; in glittery go-go dresses; and in flight on a narrow bed, rope, and swinging window, we conjure stories of outcasts who thrive against tough odds.

Without the boundless flair of public art, the telling would not be heard.

A Southeast Asian woman who lives half a block away from the Cadillac comes to a day show and then an evening show, because she just can't get enough of seeing her neighborhood lit up with beauty. A white woman from Pacific Heights who lives over a mile away comes to a day and then an evening show because she just can't get enough of seeing a neighborhood she wouldn't otherwise come to come to lit up with beauty.

Without the boundless flair of public art, the telling would not be seen.

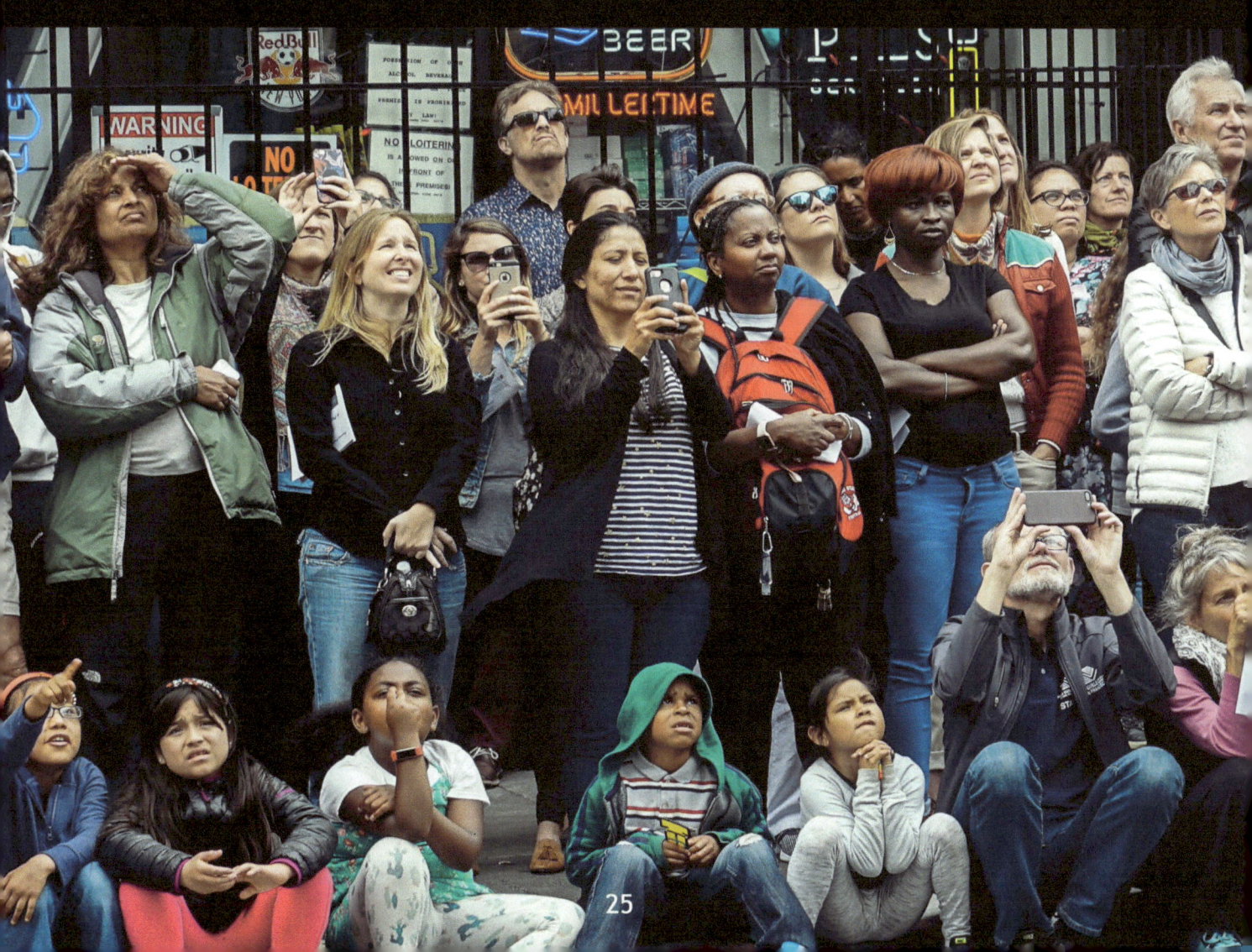

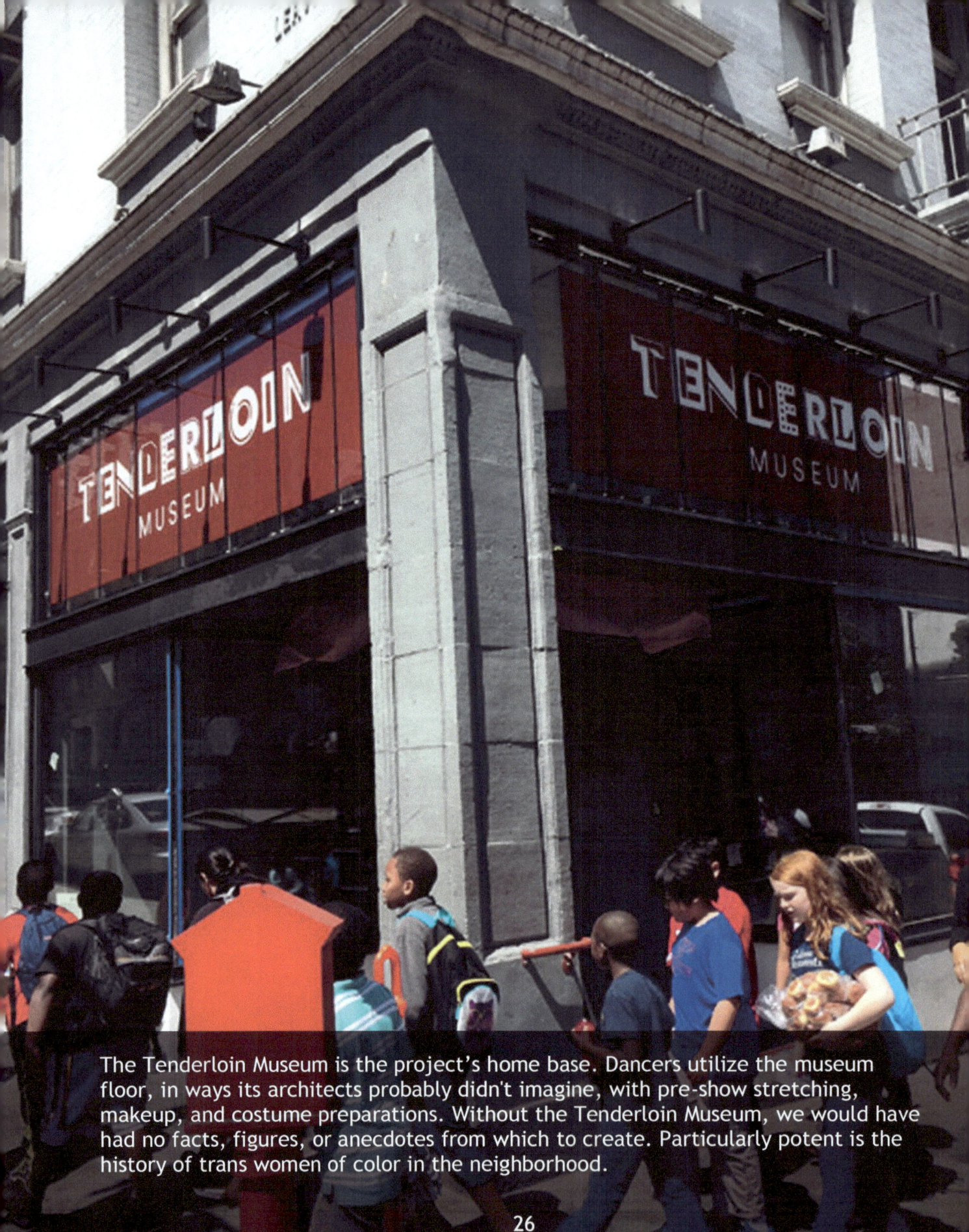

The Tenderloin Museum is the project's home base. Dancers utilize the museum floor, in ways its architects probably didn't imagine, with pre-show stretching, makeup, and costume preparations. Without the Tenderloin Museum, we would have had no facts, figures, or anecdotes from which to create. Particularly potent is the history of trans women of color in the neighborhood.

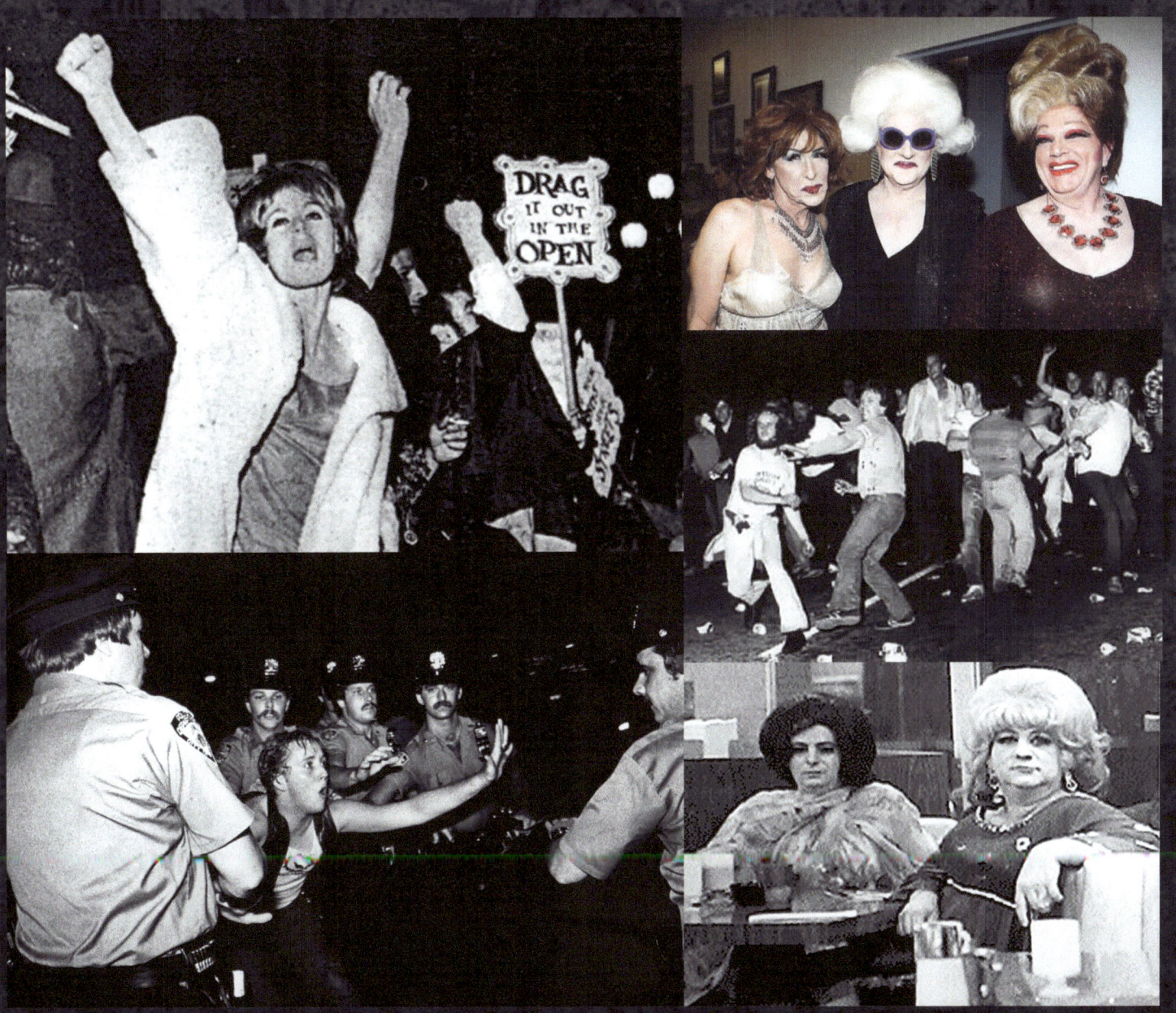

The 1960's saw the rise of activism from transgendered women (though that word didn't yet exist). Three years before the Stonewall uprising in New York, young queens of the Tenderloin were pushing back against their harsh treatment as outcasts. The Compton's Cafeteria riot was a push back against police brutality; gay and trans activists also led anti-poverty efforts of the time. We are able to tell this story with the help of performer/change-maker Honey Mahogany, a guest artist with us for the production. Wigs, gloves, bright red lipstick, a fuchsia silk robe, short skirts, and a compelling three-story fire escape help us along.

1917: Nine Ladies Dancing

Man does not like the awakening of women. He fears she will destroy civilization. And she will. Manmade civilization with its inequalities, injustices, and hatreds must go.
- A Married Woman in The Bulletin, 1917

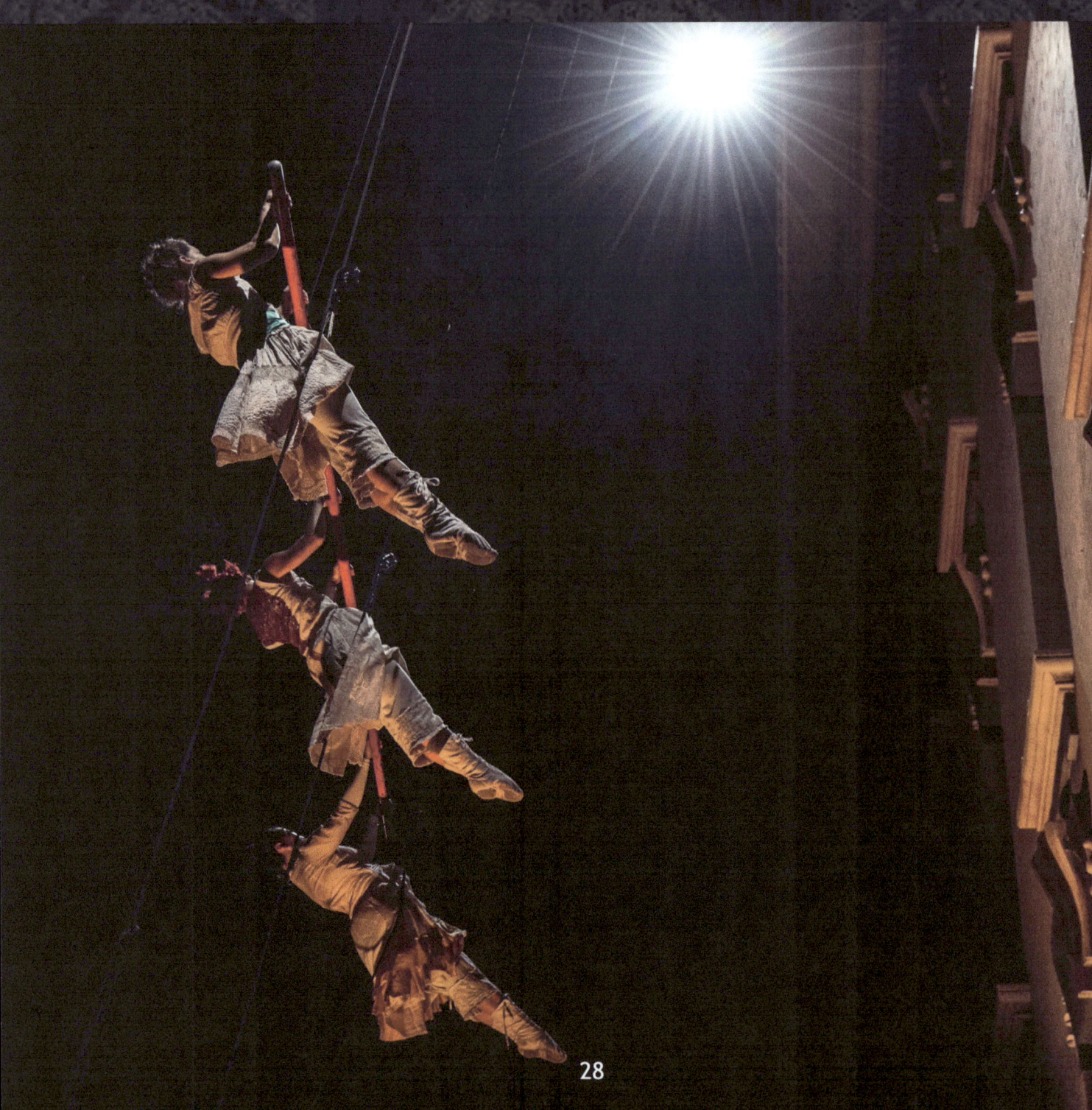

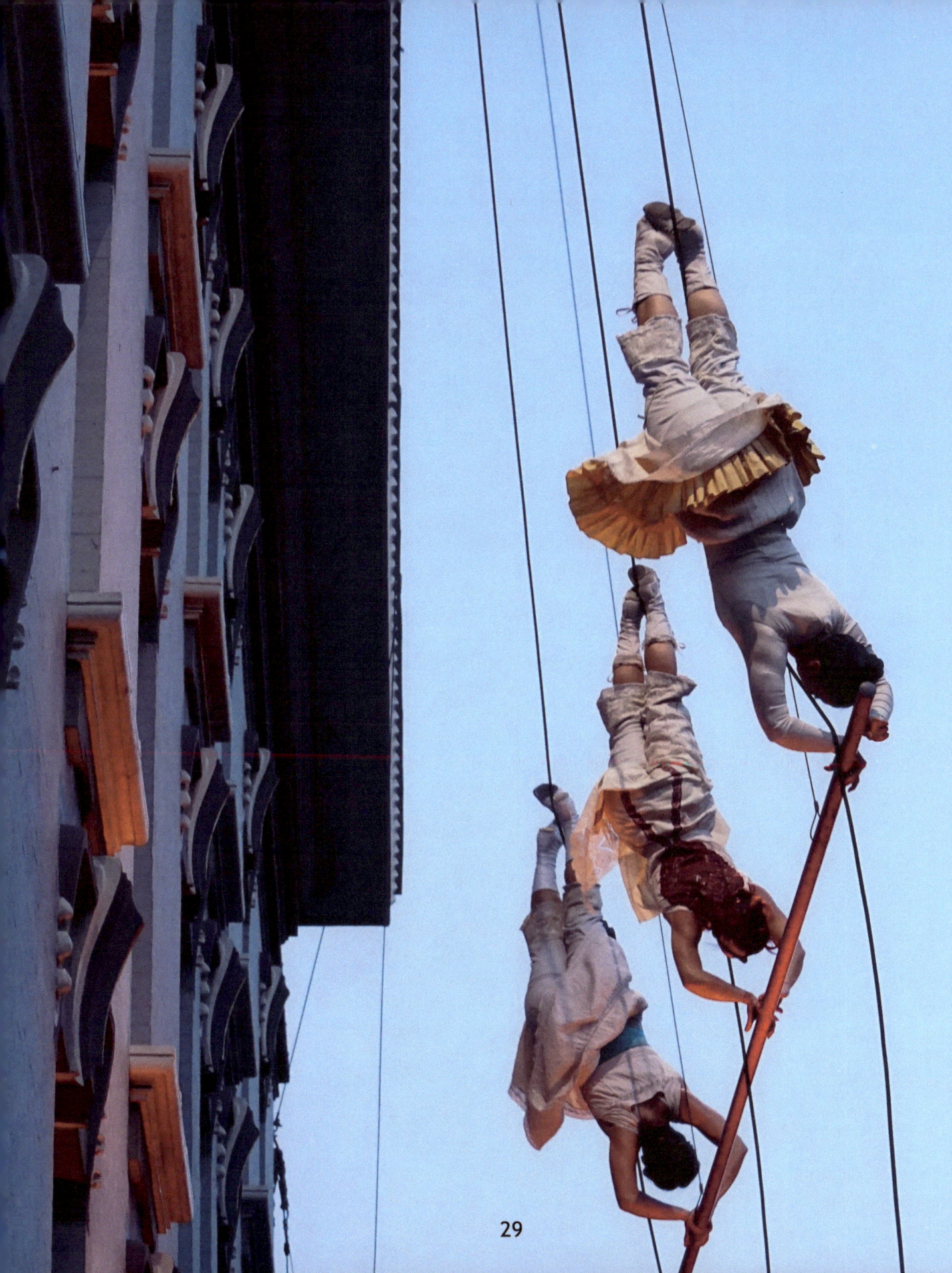

1966: The Queen's Wave

The queens of the Compton's Cafeteria Riot taught us to be brave; to be bold; to demand respect; to never take no for an answer. Without them, we would have never had a march, or a Pride, or been able to organize around the AIDS crisis. We owe our lives to them.
- Honey Mahogany, performer and change agent, 2018

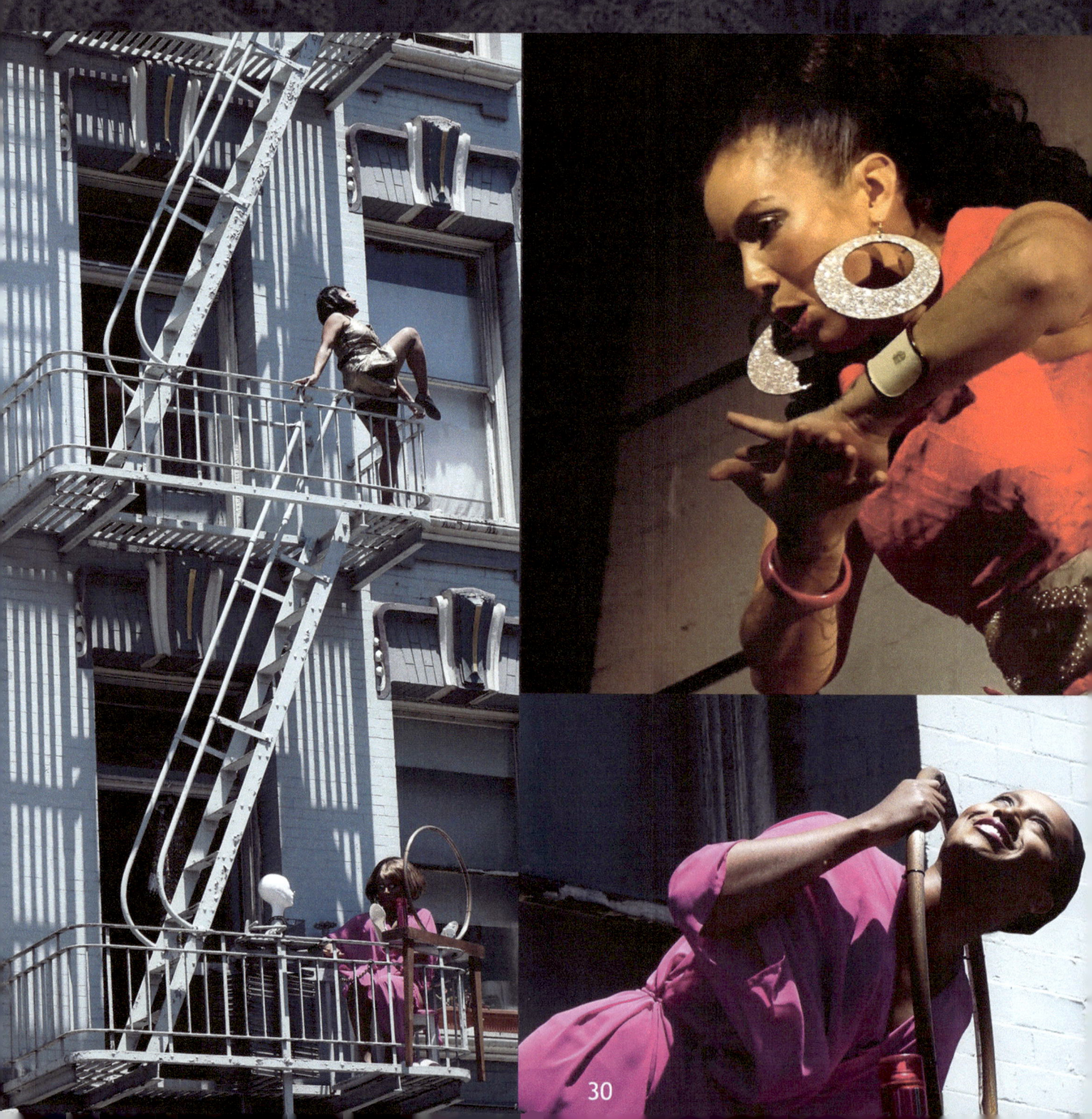

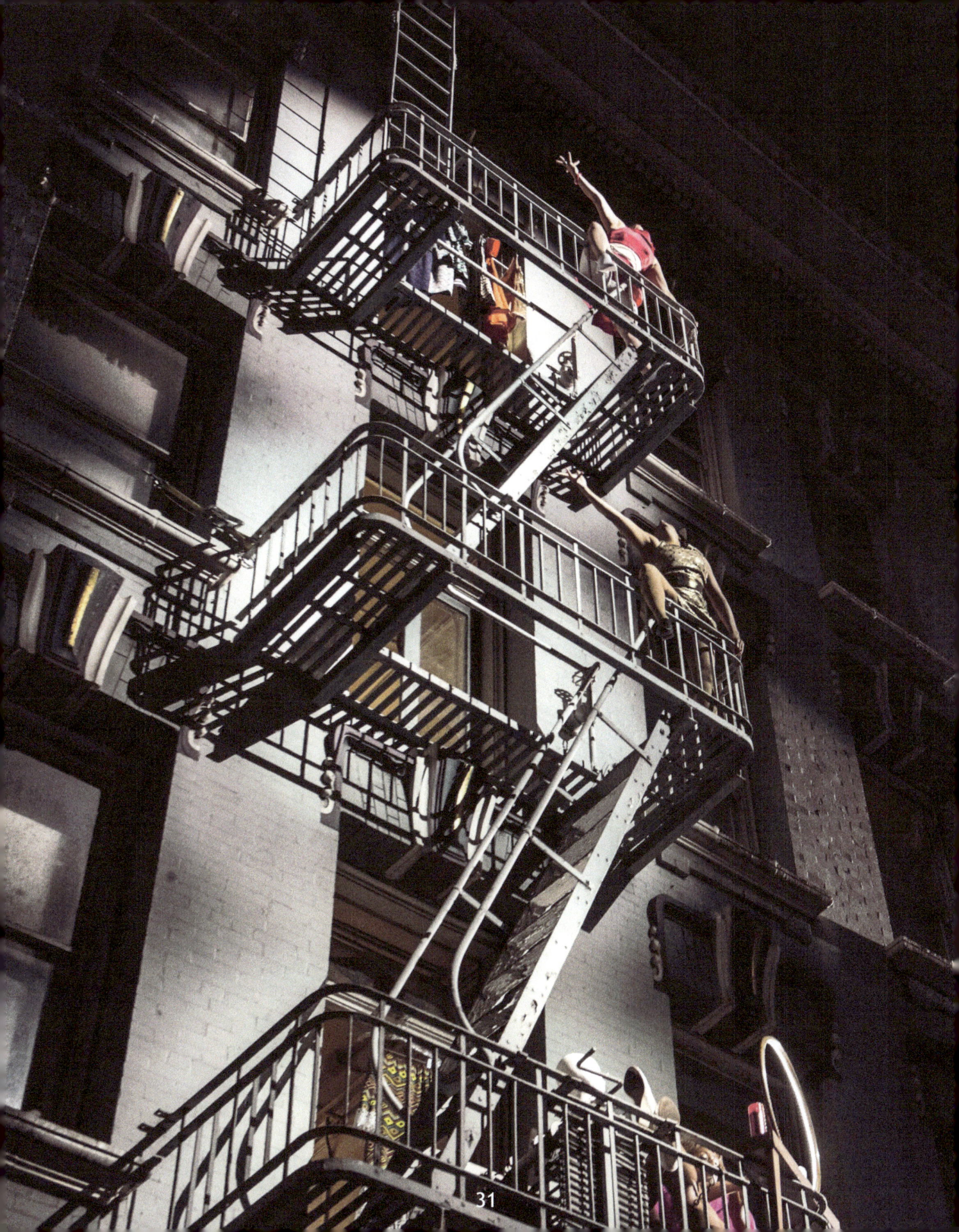

1979: This Boat

The Tenderloin is like a Lion.
- Karen Tieu, Tenderloin Resident, 2018

In this country, you have to raise your voice, ask for what you want...
- Phillip Nguyen, Southeast Asian Community Center Executive Director, 2018

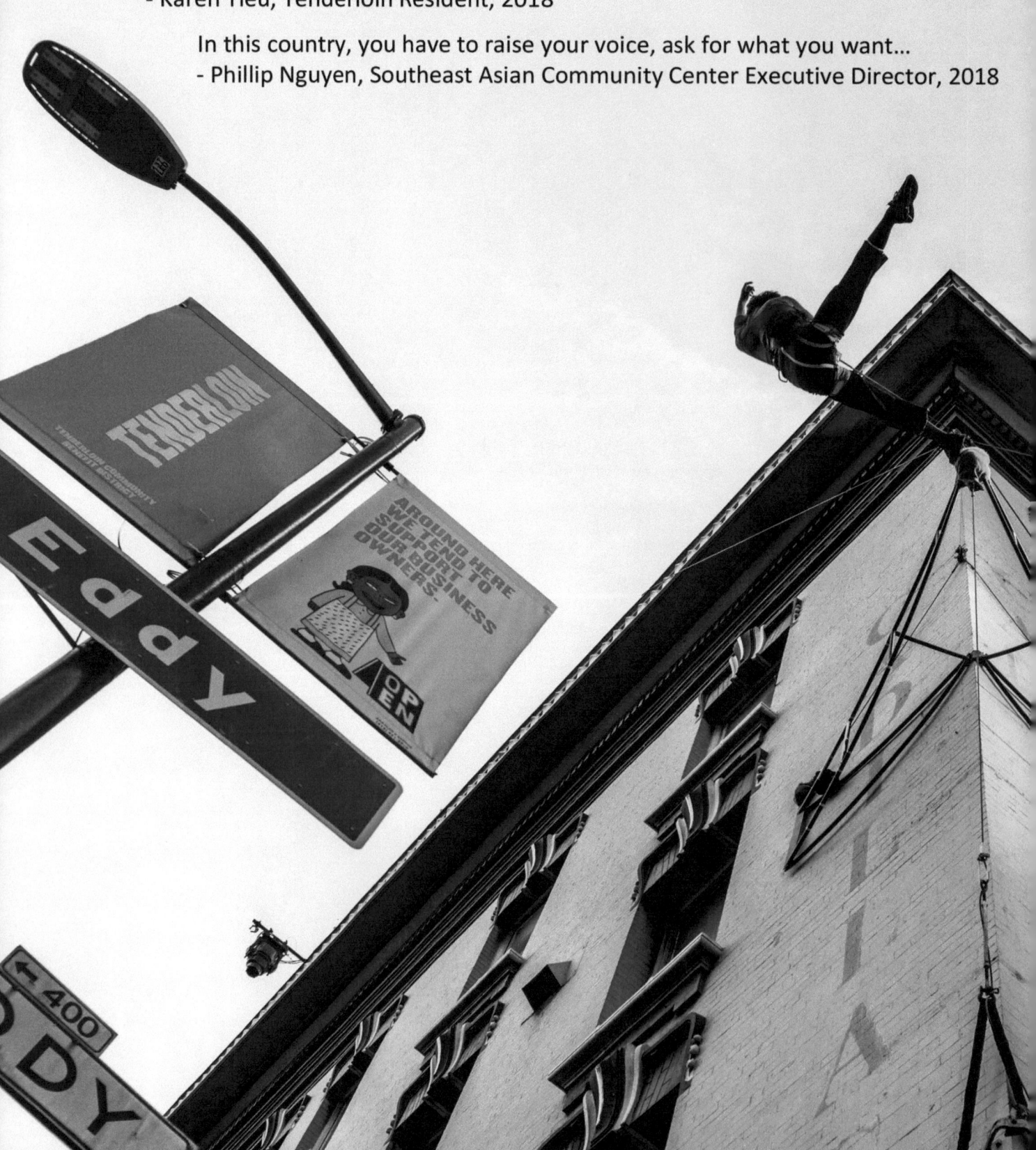

2018: Kathy's Dance

I feel like I am doing time for a crime I didn't commit, and that crime is poverty.
- Mark Parsons, Cadillac Hotel Resident, 2018

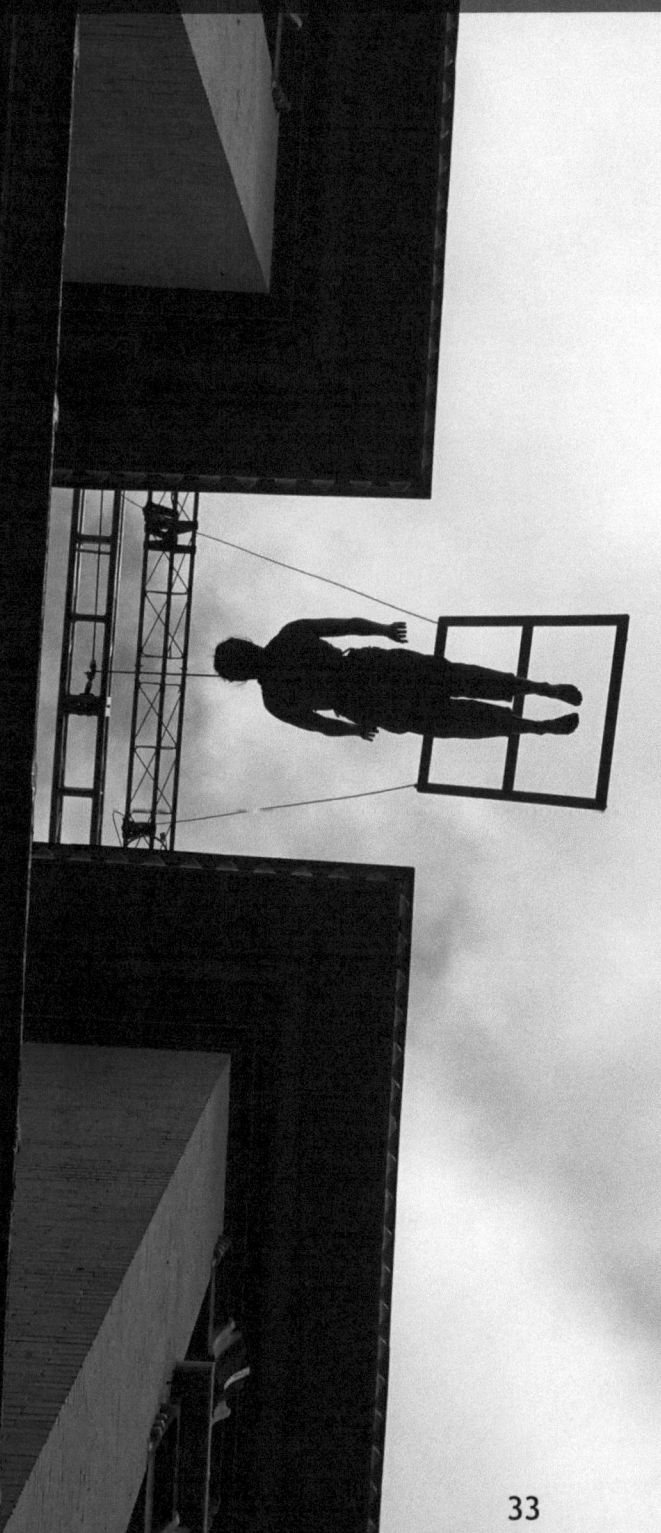

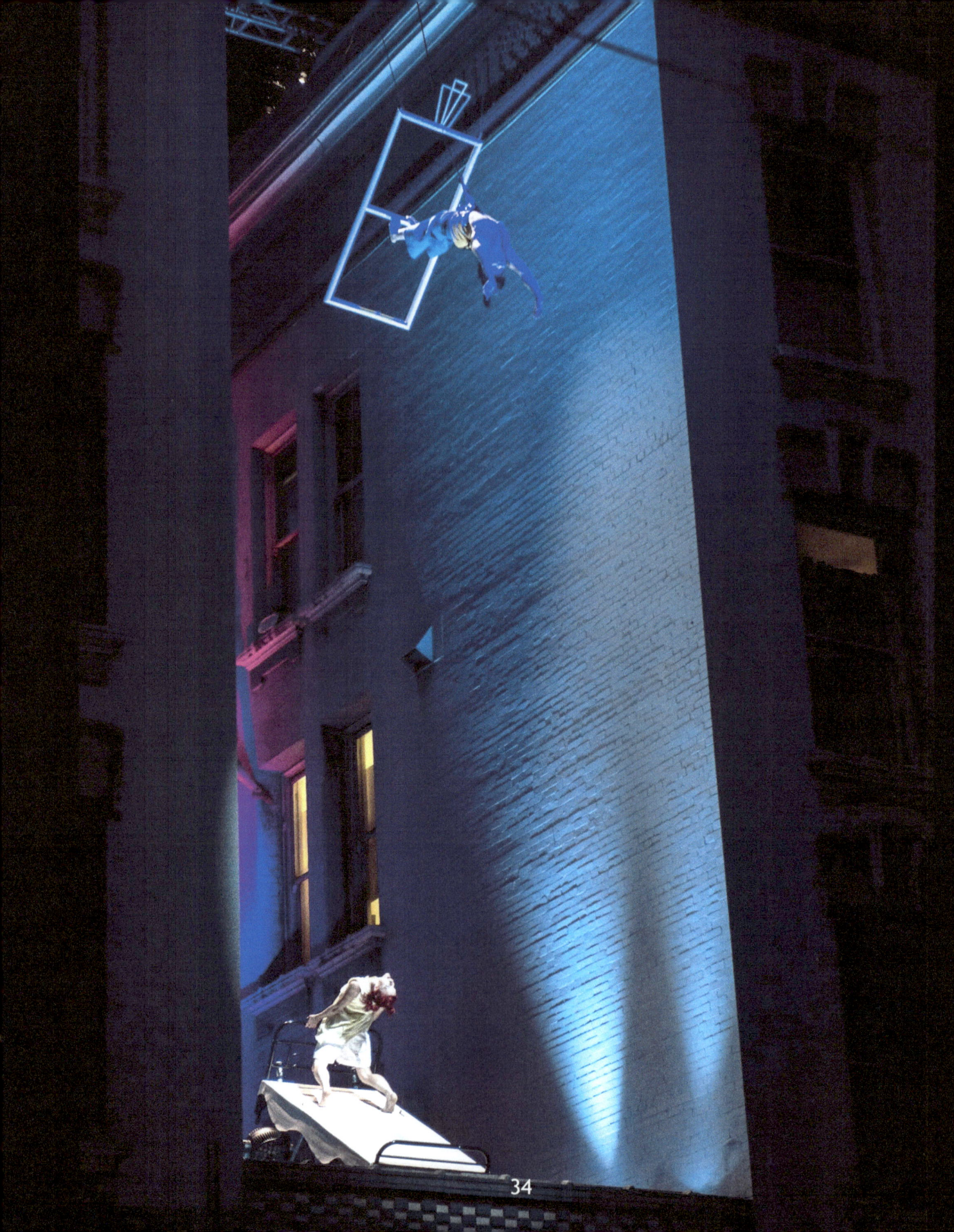

GIRLFLY in the Tenderloin

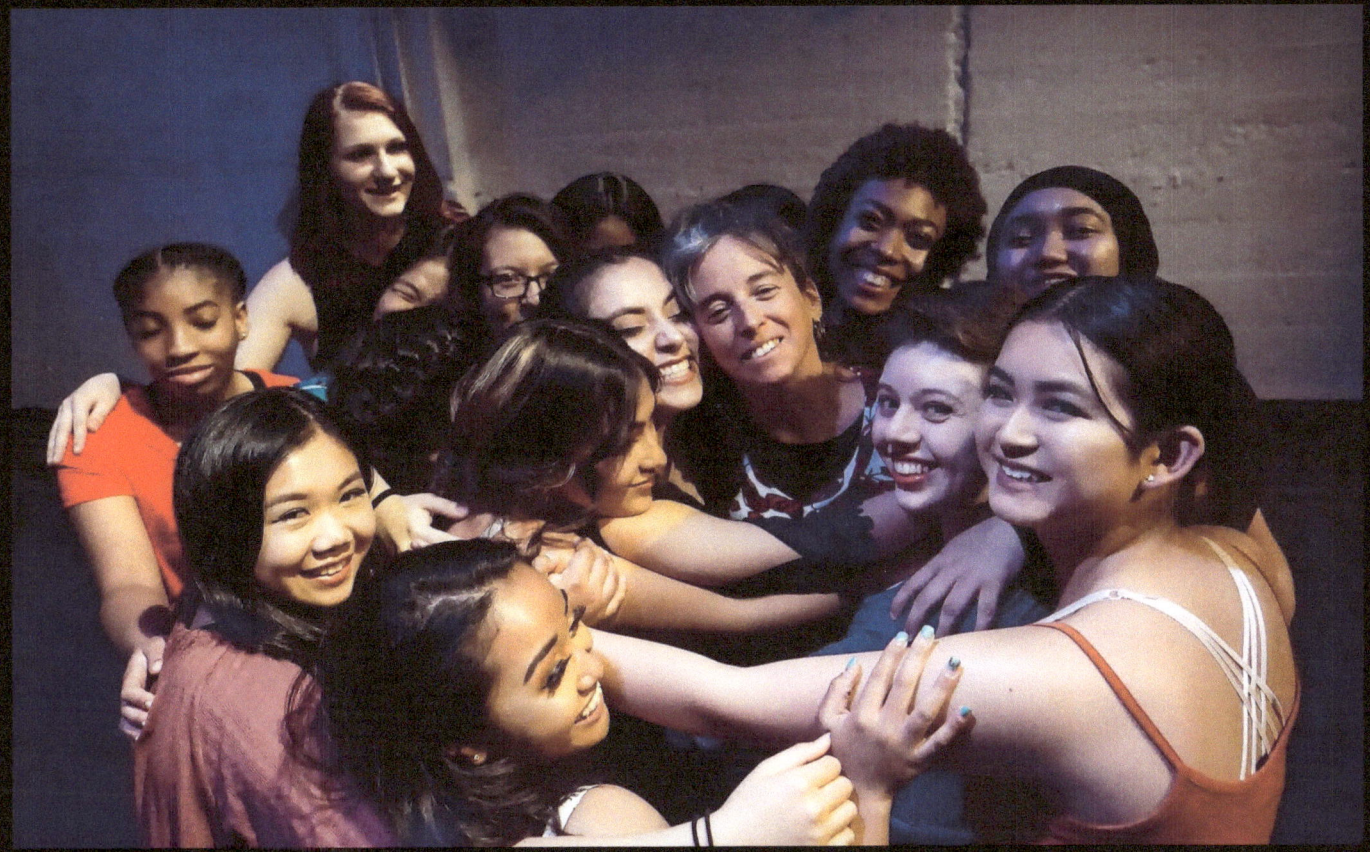

GIRLFLY is a 4-week, summer dance program for low-income girls from San Francisco. Each year, GIRLFLY facilitates an in-depth learning experience for up to 20 girls. We liken GIRLFLY to a job. The girls apply, and interview to participate. Once contracted, they attend daily dance classes and community engagement workshops for a total of 80-hours. The program culminates in two free, public performances. To promote value for their time, GIRLFLY pays each participant $500. GIRLFLY 2018 focuses on issues of importance to the Tenderloin community: immigration, workers' rights, and housing.

GIRLFLY amplifies youth voices, as it:
- Engages the body through professional dance instruction;
- Activates creativity, and leadership through dance-making;
- Teaches social awareness through advocacy projects; and
- Builds positive self-esteem through performance.

Students perform in two repertory dances created by teaching artists Jo Kreiter and Megan Lowe. The pieces focus on homelessness in the Tenderloin via the story of Mary, a current resident at the Cadillac Hotel, as well as the personal immigration story of each of six dancers who danced on a suspended boat. The girls also create a total of eight dances of their own, with music, themes and a movement vocabulary of their own choosing.

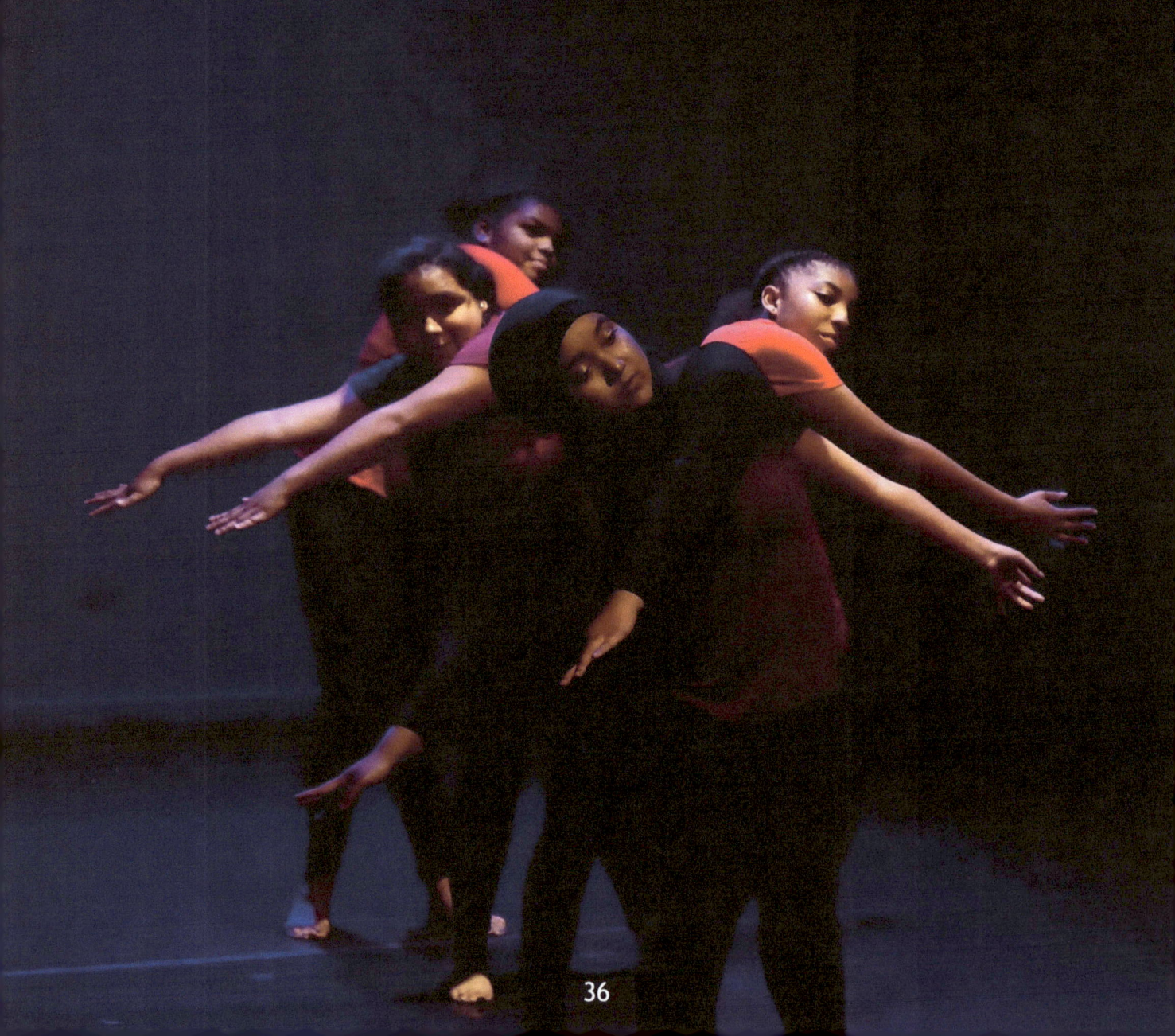

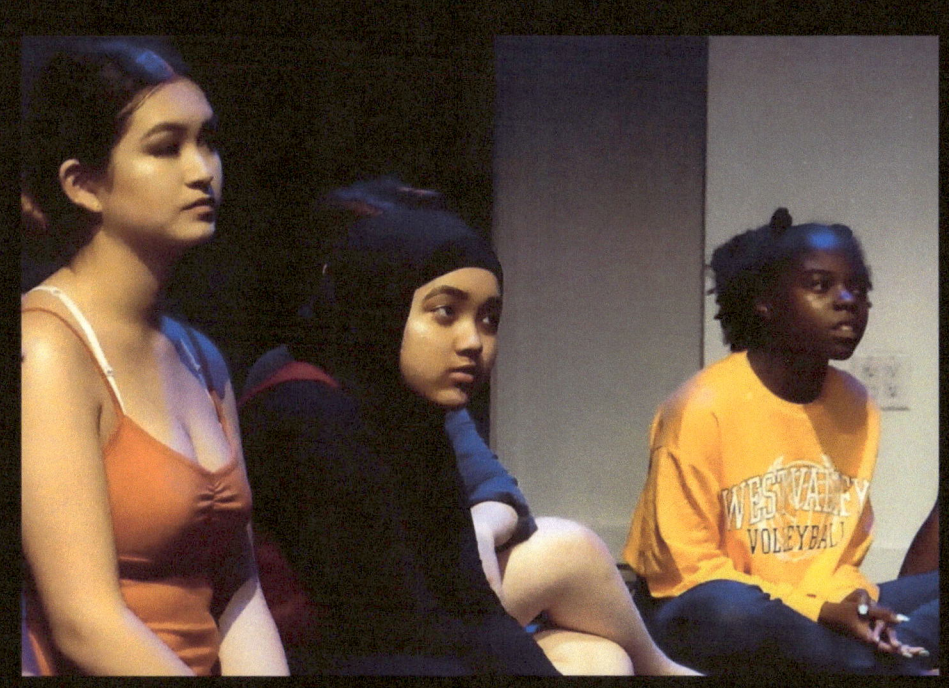
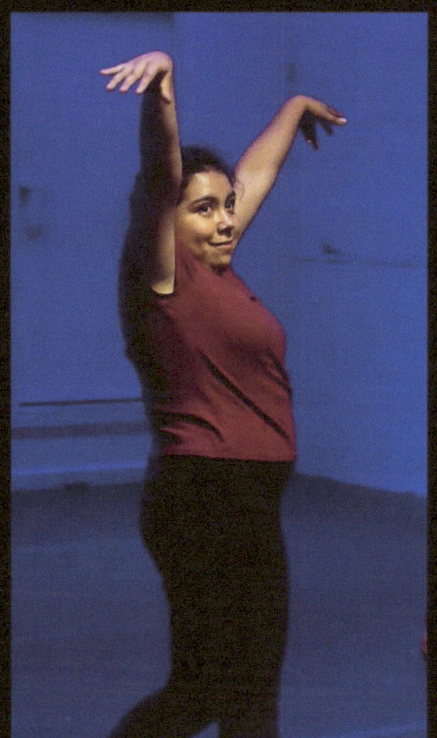

Activist Speakers in the afternoon sessions include Radhika Mishra, UNITE HERE Local 2; Pam Tau Lee, Chinese Progressive Association; Amy Lin, Aspire; and Lilla Pitman, Community Housing Partnerships.

Oral History Interviews are recorded for Ilana Master, Young Workers United; Anakh Sul Rama, Community Housing Partnerships; and Pratihba Tekkey, Tenderloin Housing Clinic.

Catherine Powell of the Labor Archives and Research Center at SF State teaches GIRLFLY students about primary source materials and the importance of documenting history of marginalized populations. She shows materials from the famed lettuce strike by CA's farm workers and shared the slogan by the women who unionized at the Lusty Lady, "Bad Girls Like Good Contracts."

Pam Tau Lee speaks of the Chinese Exclusion act as it affected her family for generations; Radhika Mishra of Unite Here Local 2 gives the girls a collective bargaining exercise to learn about wage equity; Amy Lin of Aspire speaks of her experience as an out, queer undocumented Asian youth, and gives context to displacement, policing, migration, and citizenship; Lilla Pitman of Community Housing Partnership shares her journey as a homeless youth and has the girls design their ideal urban housing situation for unhoused people.

GIRLFLY 2018 focused on issues of importance to the Tenderloin community: immigration, workers' rights, and housing.

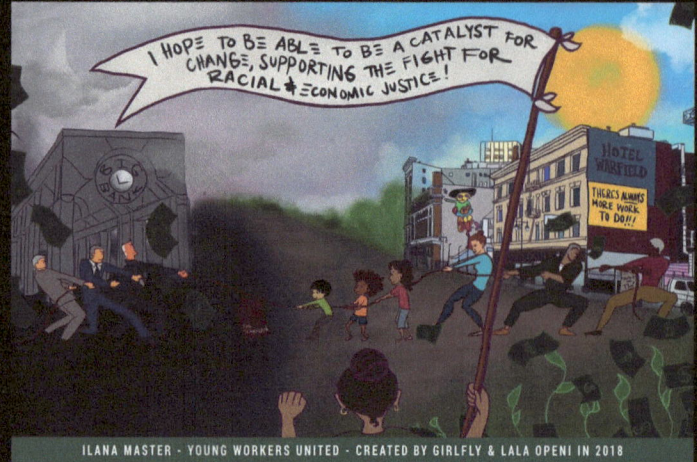

ILANA MASTER - YOUNG WORKERS UNITED - CREATED BY GIRLFLY & LALA OPENI IN 2018

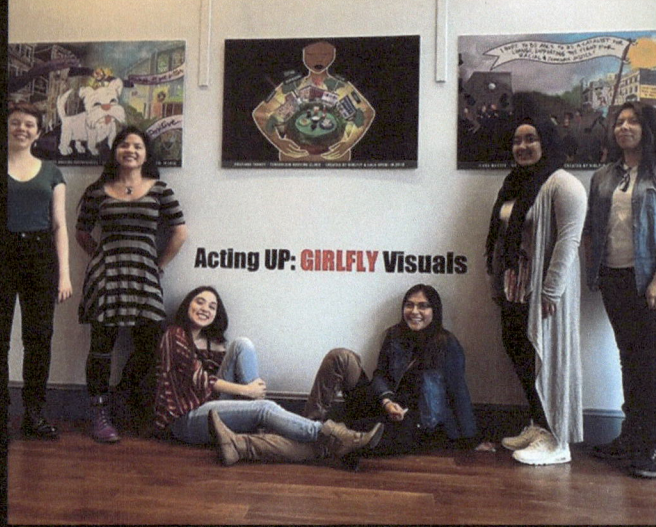

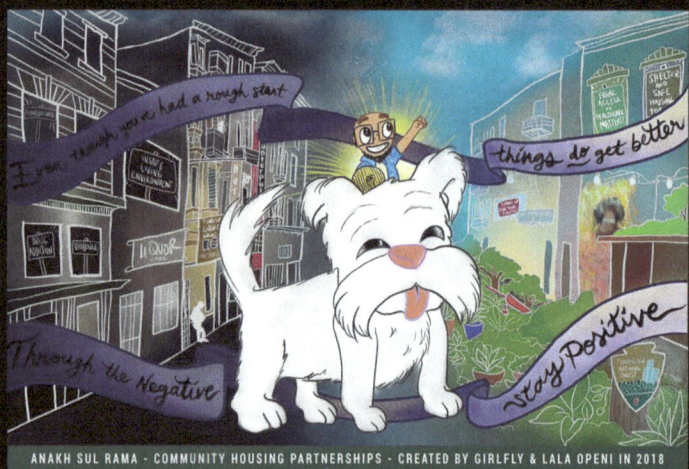

ANAKH SUL RAMA - COMMUNITY HOUSING PARTNERSHIPS - CREATED BY GIRLFLY & LALA OPENI IN 2018

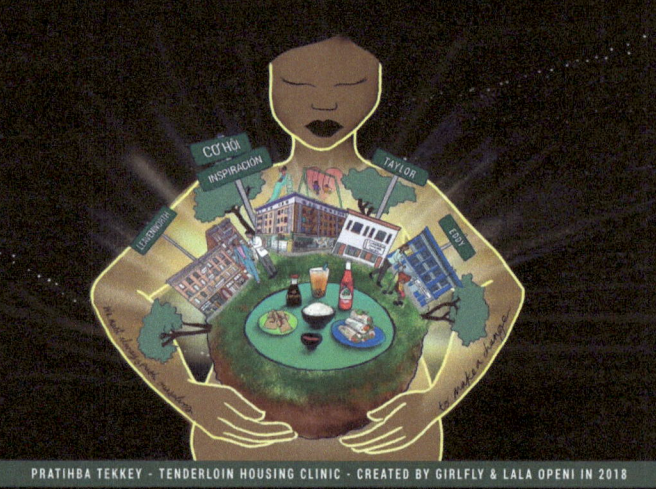

PRATIHBA TEKKEY - TENDERLOIN HOUSING CLINIC - CREATED BY GIRLFLY & LALA OPENI IN 2018

Each day, the girls (ages 14-19) hear from community activists about how real-life challenges can be surmounted by progressive social action. They discover the power of oral history to document the history of people of color, and the working class, by conducting interviews of three Tenderloin activists. The lessons of social justice activism learned over the course of GIRLFLY inform the themes of the dances choreographed by the girls. Additionally, their research culminates in a series of graphic panels created in partnership with artist Lala Openi, which are featured in a display at the Tenderloin Museum in August/September 2018.

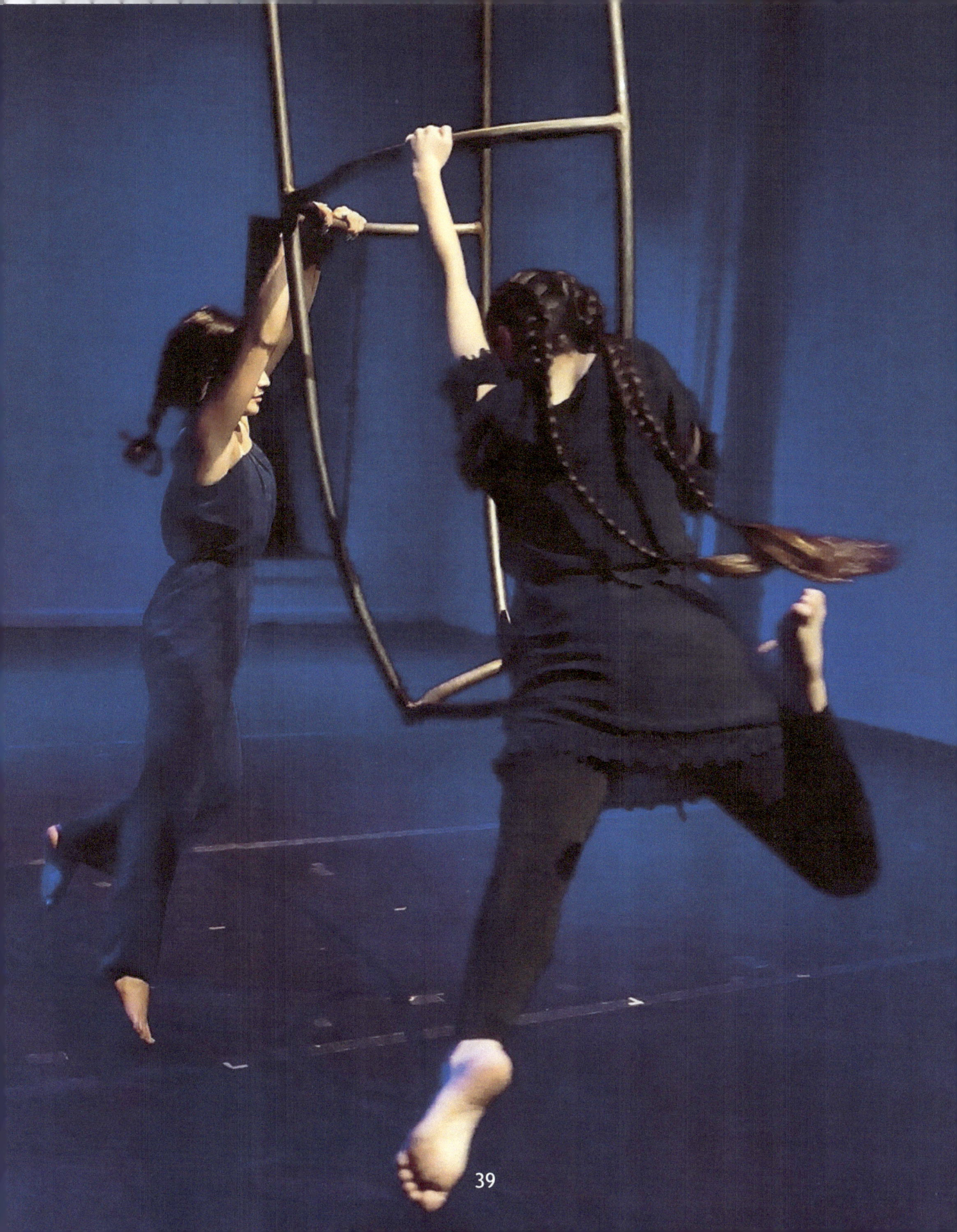

In the words of our young artists:

"GIRLFLY changed my perspective on the Tenderloin. Before it was just a neighborhood that was unsafe. Now it has history and depth."

"I learned how to make my body stronger and move in ways I was afraid to do before."

"GIRLFLY has strengthened my views on the world, particularly about the impact that women of color can have."

"I learned that immigrants can also stand up for their community."

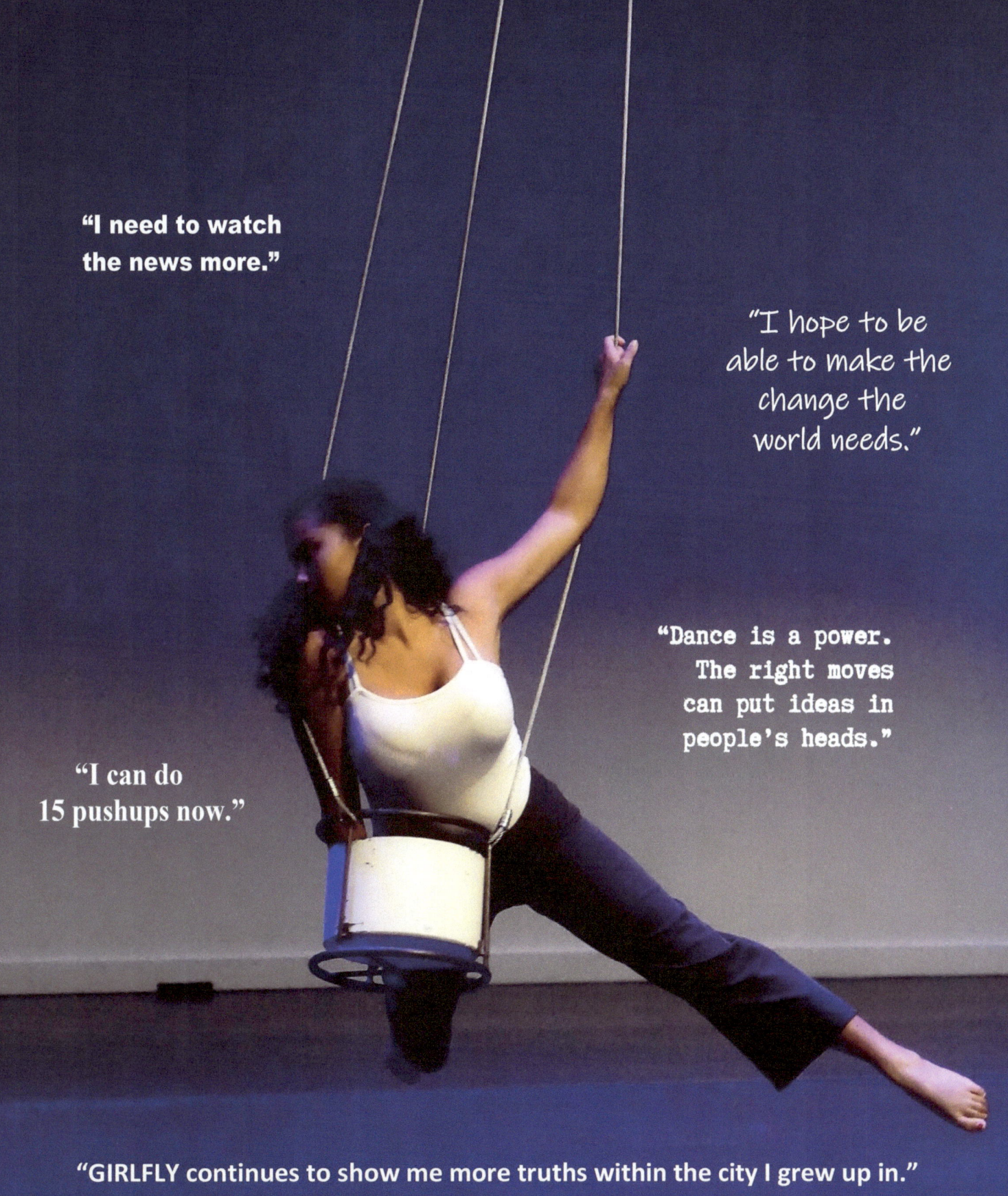

Presented by Flyaway Productions and the Tenderloin Museum
Choreography and Direction : Jo Kreiter, in collaboration with the dancers
Music : Vân Ánh Võ
Performance : Bianca Cabrera, Sonsherée Giles, MaryStarr Hope, Laura Elaine Ellis, Yayoi Kambara, Megan Lowe, & Honey Mahogany
Set Design : Sean Riley
Lighting Design : David Robertson
Costume Design : Jamielyn Duggan, Sonsherée Giles, & Miranda Caroline
Stage Manager : Pat Mahoney
Rigging Manager : Karl Gillick
Production Managers : Jack Beuttler & Cici Gruber

Flyaway Productions' Board of Directors : Joseph Blum, Deborah Gerson, R. Samuel Klatchko, Karen Tsuei, Michele Meneguez, Mary Luckey, & Jo Kreiter
Development Director : Brechin Flournoy
Social Media Marketing : Megan Lowe
Site Manager : Monica Herbert
Public Relations : John Hill
Book Design : On Paper Press

TENDER is supported by the Kenneth Rainin Foundation, Fleishhaker Foundation, National Endowment for the Arts, CA Arts Council, New Music USA, Grants for the Arts, Flyaway's generous individual donors, ZACCHO Studio's Residency Program, and the Asian Art Museum. GIRLFLY funders include the SF Department of Children, Youth and Families, the Walter and Elise Haas Fund, EILEEN FISHER, and the SF Arts Commission Innovative Partnership Program.

www.FlyawayProductions.com

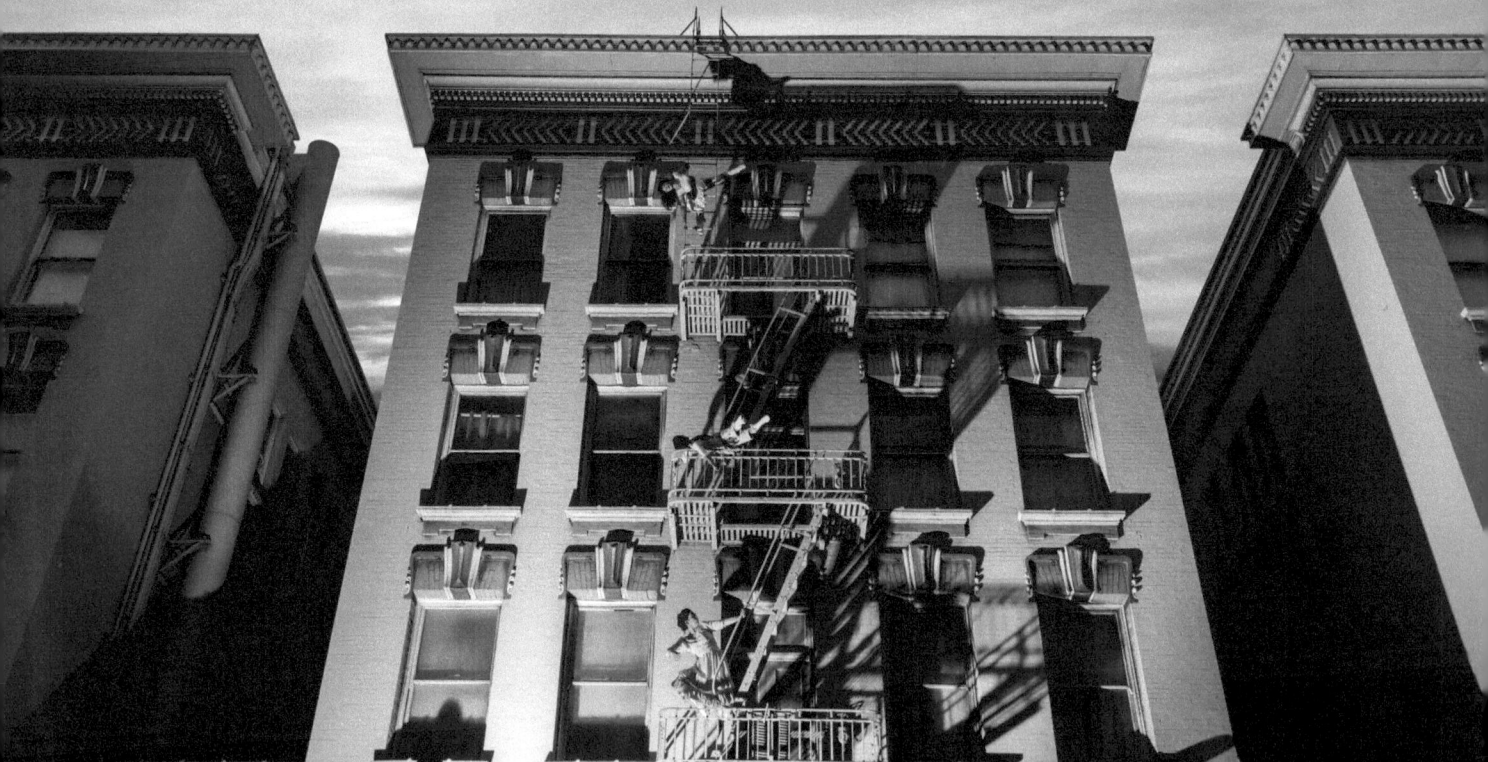